LOU BOUDREAU

COVERING ALL THE BASES

Lou Boudreau, with Russell Schneider

Sagamore Publishing
Champaign, IL 61820

Production supervision
    and book design: Brian J. Moore
Cover design: Michelle R. Dressen
Editors: David Hamburg, Russ Lake
Proofreader: Phyllis L. Bannon

Publisher's Cataloging in Publication
    (*Prepared by Quality Books Inc.*)

Boudreau, Lou, 1917-
    Covering all the bases / Lou Boudreau, Russell Schneider.
    p. cm.
    Preassigned LCCN: 93-084610.
    ISBN 0-915611-72-4

    1. Boudreau, Lou, 1917- 2. Baseball players--United States--
Biography. 3. Sportscasters--United States--Biography. 4.
Baseball--United States--Biography. I. Schneider, Russell, 1928-
II. Title.

GV865.B68B68 1993   796.357'64
                                     QBI93-855

To my wife Della, who was always at my side with her love, loyalty, and understanding, and who always wanted whatever it was that I wanted; to my family, whose love and support also provided me with incentive to succeed; and to the friends I've made along the way.

—Lou Boudreau—

To my wife Kay, for her love and encouragement, and to the remarkable man whose careers have made this book possible.

—Russell Schneider—

Contents

Acknowledgments

There are many whose help made this book possible, especially Lou Boudreau's wife Della, and their children, Barbara Golaszewski, Sharon McLain, Louis Harry Boudreau, and Jim Boudreau, and sons-in-law Denny McLain and Paul Golaszewski.

Heartfelt appreciation also is extended for the insight provided by Lou Boudreau's friends, colleagues, former players and members of the media who worked with, and covered him during his outstanding careers as a baseball player and manager, and radio commentator.

Thanks to Jack Brickhouse, Vince Lloyd and Jack Rosenberg of Station WGN in Chicago; former assistant Harry Craft, former players Bob Feller, Johnny Pesky, Joe Astroth, Gus Zernial, Bobby Shantz, and Don Bollweg; and sportswriters Peter Gammons and Cliff Keane of the *Boston Globe*, Joe McGuff of the *Kansas City Star*, Jerome Holtzman of the *Chicago Tribune*, and Hal Lebovitz and Chuck Heaton of the *Cleveland Plain Dealer*.

Special thanks to Kay Schneider, a wonderful wife (and excellent reader, editor and critic); and to two good friends, Joe Simenic, an exceptional baseball researcher, and Bill Hickey, a great writer and editor, all of whose help and support were invaluable.

Thanks, too, to Tom Kelly of American Photographic Archives, Inc. for the use of his photographs for this book, and Morris Eckhouse, executive director of the Society for American Baseball Research.

And finally my appreciation to Sagamore Publishing, especially Joe Bannon, Joe Bannon Jr., and Peter Bannon, for putting me in partnership with the man who was my idol as a youth, and now is a dear friend.

Foreword

It was 1946. My friend looked up from his sports sheet and said, "Migawd. Here it is the month of June and those crazy Red Sox haven't even lost ten games yet."

Sure enough, they were 41-9.

"Hell, they'll clinch the pennant by the first of August," he chortled.

But a funny thing happened on the way to the World Series. A guy named Lou Boudreau got a brainstorm.

Ted Williams, perhaps the greatest pure hitter of all time, stepped into the batter's box for Boston, and all of a sudden Fenway Park went crazy.

For the first time they saw what would become the famous "Boudreau Shift." Three infielders between first and second, a man in short right field and a solitary outfielder responsible for everything (or anything) hit to the left side.

"Okay, Ted, old buddy. You want to go to left? Be our guest," Boudreau and the Indians were telling the great Williams.

Further details on this radical strategy are told later in this book. My point here is that this kind of a baseball mind—Boudreau's—was a natural to analyze the game from the broadcast booth.

So, when WGN Radio in Chicago landed the Cubs' broadcasting rights, Lou Boudreau was my choice to team up with the brilliant Jack Quinlan. The brass agreed and the best radio baseball broadcasting team known up till that time was born.

After the tragic death of Quinlan, the excellence continued with Vince Lloyd and Lou at the mike for years.

What made them so good? Talent, knowledge of each man's responsibilities, and the instinct for when to talk and when to shut up.

In Lou's case, we all probably agree he's not ready for the chair of romance languages at Harvard. For that matter, what play-by-play or color man is? What we do have is a real nice guy with a tremendous knowledge of baseball who's willing to share it with listeners in understandable terms, which is exactly the way he comes across.

Lou Boudreau didn't talk down to his listeners; he didn't pat them on the head or chuck them under the chin. Nor did he grovel or bow from the waist trying to curry a favor.

He was never a second-guesser; if anything, he was a first-guesser—and he usually was right because he thought like a manager and anticipated what would be done next.

I defy any fan who listened to an entire Boudreau broadcast to tell me he didn't learn something about the game that he didn't know before.

My only complaint with Lou Boudreau was that he's a lousy handicapper. He always touted us on the wrong horses.

But he sure knew humans, especially those wearing baseball uniforms.

Jack Brickhouse
WGN Radio

****

Lou Boudreau was named manager of the Cleveland Indians in 1942, the same year I went to work for The *Plain Dealer*. So there always has been a special fondness because he was the first of many managers I got to know, and he had a warm smile and engaging personality.

In 1946, when Bill Veeck bought the Indians, he brought in some experienced help as coaches—old and wise baseball men such as Bill McKechnie, Muddy Ruel, Mel Harder and Steve O'Neill. They all contributed to the success of the Indians, but it was Boudreau who made the decisions, who ran the show.

I was doing what we called "clubhouse" stories during Boudreau's years as manager in Cleveland. It meant hustling down to the locker room after games and getting the words of wisdom from the manager, coaches, and players.

It was deadline writing after night games and Boudreau was aware of that. The clubhouse was opened quickly and so was his office. He answered our questions as openly as possible and I had the feeling he enjoyed the give-and-take with the media. His mind, which was as quick as his bat, came up with the answers and often a new angle for a story.

He was a kindly man, especially to a rookie writer. On one occasion, after I had been chastised by Bob Lemon for going to the dressing room early after he had been knocked out of a close game, Boudreau called me aside.

He could have said it differently, but instead, told me in a gentle manner, "I know you have to write in a hurry, but try to give them a little more time to cool off."

The coolness he displayed as a player both in the field and at the plate was reflected in his baseball decisions. He was more calm than the reporters the day before the pennant playoff game against the Boston Red Sox in 1948.

Then he defied the odds and came up with the unexpected but successful decision to start rookie left-hander Gene Bearden in Fenway Park. Bearden beat the Red Sox, 8-3, but it should be noted that Boudreau went 4-for-4, with two homers. It got the Indians into the World Series against the Boston Braves, whom they also beat, in six games.

There is no doubt that Boudreau, the Hall of Fame shortstop, contributed greatly to Boudreau, the manager. It was not only his play but also his inspirational leadership that took the Indians to the top.

The two qualities are difficult to separate, but as playing manager with the Indians, he gets high marks from me, just as he does for being a fine person.

I look back on Lou Boudreau's years in Cleveland, and my learning period as a sportswriter, with pleasure. It was a happy time for both of us.

Chuck Heaton
Cleveland Plain Dealer

Prologue

Among the things my mother loved were baseball, the Cleveland Indians, and Lou Boudreau, not necessarily in that order.

By the time I was old enough to read the sports pages, I, too, loved baseball, the Cleveland Indians, and Lou Boudreau, also not necessarily in that order.

One of my most vivid memories from those days is of my mother and me clipping Gordon Cobbledick's story out of the November 26, 1941, edition of the *Cleveland Plain Dealer* and pasting it in my scrapbook.

The Page One banner headline reported, "LOU BOUDREAU TO MANAGE INDIANS," and the subheads read, "Youngest Player Ever to Direct Major Club Gets 2-Year Contract," and, "Shortstop Is Surprise Choice After Bradley Fails to Find Suitable Leader Among Other Candidates; Tribe Seeks Coaches to Assist Infielder; Peckinpaugh Succeeds Slapnicka as General Manager."

It caused an argument between my mother and me that morning.

She was glad Boudreau was hired, though she probably would have been happy for an*ybody* to get the job. The Indians had finished in a fourth-place tie in 1941 and, naturally, she blamed the manager, Roger Peckinpaugh.

Isn't it always the manager's fault when a team doesn't win the pennant?

I disagreed. Not that I didn't like Boudreau. I did. The fact is, Boudreau was tied with Hal Trosky, Mel Harder, and Bob Feller as my favorite players. But that was the very reason I argued that hiring Boudreau was not a good thing.

If I'd been as baseball-wise then as I thought I was, I would have expressed my objection better. I would have said that managers are hired to be fired—in the vernacular of today's sportswriters—and when the time comes for Boudreau to be fired, we will lose a wonderful shortstop.

Six years later I could have said, "I told you so," when Bill Veeck planned to trade Boudreau because he wanted a new manager. I guess the reason I didn't was that my mother was so upset, as were most true Indians fans in Cleveland.

My mother was not normally a contentious woman, but she was that winter of 1947-48, when Veeck tried to justify the proposed deal that would bring Vernon Stephens to play shortstop and Jimmy Dykes to manage the Indians.

Both of us joined the protest by clipping out the "Boudreau Ballot" that appeared daily on the front page of the Cleveland News, giving fans the opportunity to vote their approval or disapproval of the deal.

Boudreau "won," of course. By a landslide. And Veeck, always sensitive to passions of the ticket-buying public, called off the deal and kept Boudreau the shortstop and, thus, Boudreau the manager.

It was a decision only the other seven teams in the American League regretted, especially the Boston Red Sox, who were beaten by the Indians—and especially by Boudreau—in an unprecedented one-game playoff for the pennant.

Boudreau was magnificent. It is doubtful that any one player ever made a greater physical or inspirational impact on his team than Boudreau did on the Indians in that 1948 season.

It is still regularly referred to in Cleveland as the "golden year" of the Indians, who have had precious few of them.

Boudreau and the Indians couldn't do it again in 1949 and 1950, and he was fired. By then his marvelous skills as a shortstop and a hitter were on the wane. The years had taken their toll on Boudreau's body, especially his ankles, which were weak from the time he led his high school basketball team to the Illinois state championship finals three years in a row.

A year later, except for four at-bats into 1952, Boudreau's playing career would end—but not his managerial career—though his deeds would not be forgotten.

As then-Commissioner Bowie Kuhn said at the time of Boudreau's 1970 induction into the Hall of Fame:

"The most remarkable thing about this remarkable man was the way he stretched the wonderful skills he had into superlative skills. As a shortstop he was a human computer, he knew all the hitters' habits, he knew all the moves of the base runners, he knew what the pitcher was going to pitch, he had an instinct for where the ball would be hit, and from all of this he fashioned the wonderful ball player that we knew as Lou Boudreau in the major leagues."

The record book confirms Kuhn's testimonial. Boudreau won the American League batting championship with a .327 average in 1944, was elected the AL's Most Valuable Player in 1948 when he batted .355, appeared in seven All-Star games and managed the AL to an 11-7 victory over the National League in 1949, tied a record by leading AL shortstops in fielding percentage eight years, and finished his thirteen-year playing career with a .295 lifetime average in 1,646 games.

And then, as Kuhn also said on the steps of the Hall of Fame in Cooperstown on July 27, 1970, Boudreau went "into a second career as one of America's finest baseball play-by-play sportscasters."

Little wonder that I was thrilled to be Boudreau's co-author for this book.

His story is a remarkable one, but then—as I told my mother a long time ago—Lou Boudreau was a remarkable player who became a remarkable manager.

And he's more a favorite of mine now than he ever was.

Russell Schneider
Cleveland, Ohio

Thank You, Mr. Martin

How different my life and career would have been if I had not written that letter to Alva Bradley and dropped it in the mailbox outside George Huff Gymnasium at the University of Illinois the night of November 20, 1941.

Or if I had been able to retrieve it when the second thoughts began.

Would Mr. Bradley laugh? Ridicule me? Would he tell anybody, or just throw the letter away?

I felt pretty dumb. Even now, more than fifty years later, I look back and realize it was a very brash thing for me to do. And if I had it to do over I probably wouldn't have, though I have no regrets now.

Even my wife Della thought it was foolish of me to think that I would even be considered to manage the Cleveland Indians. There I was, twenty-four years old, fresh out of college, probably the youngest guy on the Indians team, with less than three seasons in the major leagues, thinking I could handle a job that men twice my age were unable to do.

Did I say brash? How about cocky. Even stupid. Pick one.

But I'm glad now that I had enough confidence in myself then and that I was bold enough to believe I could manage a group of older, experienced players and continue to be a productive player myself.

Still, if I could have reached into that mailbox and retrieved my letter to Mr. Bradley, the owner of the Indians, I know I would have done so.

I entered the gym and told the two men I was helping coach the university basketball and baseball teams what I'd done and asked if they knew how I could get my letter back.

Doug Mills, the head basketball coach, wanted to know why I'd written the letter. I said I wanted to be a major league manager someday and I figured I may as well start now while there was an opening at Cleveland.

I'd read in the paper that the Indians were looking for a manager to replace Roger Peckinpaugh, who was being promoted to general manager because of the resignation of C. C. Slapnicka. I felt qualified—at least when I wrote the letter—because I'd been captain of my high school basketball team as a sophomore, junior, and senior; captain of my college basketball team my junior year when seniors usually get that job; and at the time was freshman baseball and basketball coach at Illinois.

Brash or not, I was confident of my ability.

Wally Roettger, who'd played for several National League teams and was the head baseball coach at Illinois, chuckled and told me to stop worrying. He said Mr. Bradley probably would just throw my letter in the wastebasket anyway.

It made me feel better, though I admit I was a little disappointed, too.

The truth is, deep down inside I did feel capable of managing the Indians. I'd played under two Cleveland managers, Oscar Vitt in 1939 and 1940, and Peckinpaugh in 1941, and while I respected both men, I felt I could do the job without it hurting my ability to play shortstop.

But I took Roettger's advice and concentrated on my job as coach of the Illinois freshman basketball players who, two years later, would become famous as the "Whiz Kids," one of the best college teams in the country.

I put my letter out of my mind, but three days later—on November 23, 1941—I got a long-distance telephone call. It was from Mr. Bradley. He'd received my letter and invited me to meet with the Indians' board of directors to tell them why I thought I could manage the team.

I was shocked. And the truth be told, suddenly I didn't want to go. I assumed Mr. Bradley was just being courteous, that as long as I was a member of the Indians organization, he felt he owed me the opportunity to be interviewed. I told him I'd let him know, and once again I went to Doug and Wally for advice.

They chuckled at my nervousness and told me to stop worrying. They said the experience of being interviewed would be good for me, that it would be helpful down the road. Neither of them took Mr. Bradley's invitation seriously.

Della wished me luck, but told me I'd be making a mistake to get my hopes up (which of course I didn't). She also said that, in the unlikely possibility I'd be offered the job, it would be a mistake to take it because it would be too much for me to play shortstop and manage the team.

The next day I was on a train for Cleveland, still concerned that I'd be making a fool of myself.

The interview was held November 24 in the Marion Building, a few blocks up the road from the Cleveland Stadium. I was told later that two other men were interviewed ahead of me. One I know was Burt Shotton, who previously had managed the Philadelphia Phillies. I never found out the name of the other candidate.

When it was my turn to meet the directors, they fired questions at me for more than two hours. Mainly they wanted to know how I would handle things if this or that happened, and if being manager of the team might affect my playing.

They also asked several times why I thought I could be a good manager, as young as I was and with as little experience as I'd had in professional baseball, and if my playing and managing might lead to dissension among the rest of the men on the team.

I told them I'd majored in physical education in college with the intention of going into coaching, that I'd been captain of my basketball team at Illinois, and was confident I could handle the players, as well as the newspapermen covering the Indians. There wasn't much radio coverage then, and no television, of course, so that was no problem then, though it certainly is now.

The directors told me to wait outside the meeting room, which I did, all the while thinking I wasn't going to get the job— and convincing myself that it would be just as well if I didn't.

I kept thinking about the question they'd asked over and over, if being manager of the team would affect my playing. I didn't think it would, but who really knew?

My first two full seasons with the Indians were pretty good; I hit .295 and drove in 101 runs in 155 games in 1940, and .257 in 148 games in 1941. Both years I made the American League All-Star team.

The thought kept running through my mind, if I failed as a manager, I'd still be young enough to keep on playing. But if I failed as a player, then I'd have a real problem, though it wasn't enough to change my mind.

I really wanted the job. It had become a challenge that I was anxious to face.

Finally I was called back into the conference room. Some of the directors greeted me with a smile, though most of them, including Mr. Bradley, looked very stern.

"Lou," Mr. Bradley said, "We have agreed to let you manage the team, that perhaps a younger man might be what is needed around here."

I could hardly believe it. I felt like jumping on the table and singing. My salary was to be $25,000, $20,000 as manager, and $5,000 as a player—but the money didn't really matter. I would have accepted anything.

Then Mr. Bradley said, "There is one stipulation. We want you to hire older, experienced coaches to help you." They recommended that I start with Shotton, who was favored by several of the directors before they chose me, and I think they felt they owed him a job. Of course, I agreed.

Shotton was a good man, though I sometimes had the impression he doubted my ability because of my age and inexperience. He was 57 at the time and had managed the Phillies for six years, beginning in 1928 when I was only in the fifth grade. Later there were times that I think Shotton resented me because I got the job instead of him, though we got along well enough, and he always did what I asked.

I also hired Oscar Melillo, a former major league infielder and an old friend who lived near my home in Harvey, Illinois, and George Susce, a former catcher who played briefly in the major leagues, though mostly in the minors.

Melillo also was quite a bit older, 42, but I'd known him from times we'd been together at banquets, he as a local boy who made good in the major leagues, and me as a good high school and college athlete, which I was, especially in basketball.

I wanted Susce, who was nicknamed "Good Kid," to be in charge of my bullpen. He got along well with everybody.

Later I learned how close I came to not getting the job, and the identity of the man I had to thank for convincing the other directors to hire me, for convincing them that a young manager might indeed be what the Indians needed.

It was Mr. George Martin. I'll never forget him. He was the chairman of the board of the Sherwin-Williams Co. in Cleveland.

The other members of the board, in addition to Alva Bradley, were his brother Charles, John Sherwin, Sr., Oris T. and Mantis J. Van Sweringen, Joseph Hostetler, Newton D. Baker, George Tomlinson, Percy Morgan, I. F. Freiberger, and Eben G. Crawford. A thirteenth director had been the late Huey P. Long, a U.S. senator from Louisiana.

The Indians had three managers in the previous five years. All were veteran, experienced men—Steve O'Neill, who was fired in 1937; Oscar Vitt, who ran the club from 1938 through 1940 before he was fired; and Peckinpaugh in 1941—and all three had different personalities and styles, which probably was a factor in the decision to hire me.

O'Neill was a cheerful, personable Irishman who was easy to get close to and like. Vitt was intense, often volatile, hard to understand and harder to get to know. Peckinpaugh was laid back, quiet, a genuinely nice man.

In retrospect, I believe the directors decided they wanted a middle-of-the-road type manager, someone who was neither as jovial and outgoing as O'Neill, nor as introverted and tough as Vitt, nor as outgoing and pleasant as Peckinpaugh.

Cleveland had become infamous throughout baseball as the "graveyard of managers" because so many men had so much trouble, and the Indians had won only one pennant, in 1920, in the 41 years they'd been in the American League.

But none of that bothered me, probably because I was too young to know better.

I was told that the directors initially voted 11-1 against hiring me. Mr. Martin was the only one who voted for me. But then, in the next 30 minutes, he changed those 11 no's to 11 yes's. I'll always be grateful to Mr. Martin, who was quite elderly and passed away before I was able to prove to him that his judgment had been good. Several years later Mrs. Martin told me that her husband would have been very proud of me, which was nice to hear.

After the meeting and the directors' decision to hire me, Mr. Bradley told me to go back to my hotel room and not talk on the phone or see anybody until the next day, when I would be introduced as the Indians' new manager in a press conference.

But I did make one phone call. It was to Della. She, of course, was surprised—very surprised—but elated, just as I was.

Della never dreamed I'd get the job, not because she lacked confidence in me, but because of my age. She wasn't alone.

But thanks to George Martin, I did.

The Way It
All Began

I didn't sleep well that night, my first night as manager of the Cleveland Indians.

Not that I was scared or doubted my ability, but a thousand thoughts kept racing through my mind.

Most of them were about my parents, especially my dad, who had died in 1939. He's the one who instilled in me a love for baseball and, more than anyone else, helped me develop the athletic ability that got me, first, a basketball scholarship to the University of Illinois, and then into professional baseball.

My dad, Louis Boudreau, Sr., had been a minor league and semi-pro third baseman near Kankakee, Illinois. He was pretty good, though not good enough to make a career of baseball. He worked most of his adult life as a machinist in Harvey.

He also was a great fan of the Chicago Cubs, and made me one, too. When I was eight or nine years old, my dad started taking me to Cubs games a couple of times a month and I kept a scorebook on their games from the radio broadcasts. My favorites were Riggs Stephenson, Woody English, Stan Hack, and Billy Jurges.

I was a catcher when I started playing as a kid, and I was pretty good. I liked catching because I liked being in the game for every pitch and with every play taking place in front of me.

I switched to third base because of my father. He said he could help me more because that was the position he'd played, and also that I'd last longer in the game if I didn't catch because

I wouldn't be getting hurt so often. My dad and I, with my older brother Albert, would go to the school yard almost every night and play our own special game. Dad would hit me a hundred grounders and Albert would keep score of how many I fielded cleanly. Albert also liked baseball but wasn't very good at it.

It was my dad who also instilled in me the determination to excel, especially when a new challenge was presented.

He would have been so proud of me that day George Martin convinced the Indians directors to hire me.

My parents divorced when I was seven years old. It made it difficult for all of us. I'd live with my dad at my grandmother's house for a while, then go to live with my mother and her new husband, a man named Joe Trenticosti. We got along all right, though he didn't pay much attention to me. He was a shoemaker and wasn't interested in sports.

I was living with my mother and stepfather when I went to Thornton Township High School in Harvey. Thornton didn't have a baseball team, but I earned four letters in basketball. We won the state championship my sophomore year, which was a big thrill for me, and went to the finals the next two years. It helped me get a scholarship to Illinois in the summer of 1935.

I wasn't a big scorer, but I was a good playmaker and passer. And though I wasn't especially fast, I was quick. But I always had problems with my ankles, even back in high school. They bothered me throughout my career and I had to tape them before every game I played. They were so weak, I sometimes felt like taping them before I went to a dance.

One of my prized mementos is my high school basketball uniform, which Thornton "retired." They even gave me my old locker. It's now in my recreation room—with my Thornton uniform hanging inside—next to the American League Most Valuable Player award I won in 1948.

The most important thing that happened to me in high school was that I met Della—her maiden name was DeRuiter—and she's been my "girl" ever since. We were married June 5, 1938, after I finished my junior year at Illinois.

That also was after I experienced one of the most difficult periods of my life, during a time that should have been a highlight of my college career.

Everything went well my first three years at Illinois. I belonged to the Phi Sigma Kappa fraternity and had a job washing pots and pans that helped pay some bills. My grades weren't anything to brag about, but I was getting along okay in my classes, majoring in physical education and doing well on both the baseball and basketball teams.

Freshmen weren't allowed to play varsity sports in those days, but I was a two-year starter in basketball and as a third baseman in baseball. We were Big Ten co-champion with Minnesota in 1938, the last season I played baseball at Illinois.

Basketball was my best game then. I wasn't a real good hitter in baseball, my average was around .275, .280, but I was good in the field and made All-Big Ten both years. Both of my coaches, Wally Roettger in baseball and Doug Mills in basketball, were very good influences on me.

It was Mills who helped get me a scholarship to Illinois on my basketball ability. He had been a high school coach at Elgin, Illinois, and I'd played against his teams when I was at Thornton.

I'm also grateful to Jack Lipe, my baseball coach and athletic director at Thornton Township High School, and Dr. J. D. Logsdon, who was like a second father to me. Dr. Logsdon was the superintendent at Whittier Elementary School in Harvey and, not only was he my first coach, he also followed my career through high school, college, and in professional baseball. The values I learned from both of them were important throughout my career in sports.

Though basketball and baseball were my games at the University of Illinois, I also was on the varsity football team under Coach Bob Zuppke in the fall of 1937—but only for two days.

Zuppke had seen me play quarterback and kick for my fraternity team when we won the intramural touch football championship. He wasn't impressed by my passing ability but liked what he saw of my placekicking. He invited me to come out for the varsity. I thought it would be neat and got permission from my baseball and basketball coaches, who said it would be okay if I only kicked—which is all I wanted to do, and all that Coach Zuppke wanted.

The first day I was out with the team Zuppke sent me to a practice field with a third-string center to snap the ball, a third-string quarterback to hold the ball, and two managers to retrieve my kicks and keep track of how many would have been good.

We were out there for two hours straight, until about 6 o'clock, when it started to get dark. But that didn't stop us. At least it didn't stop Coach Zuppke. He apparently got mad at the rest of the squad and ordered the field lights turned on. We practiced for about two more hours.

That night back at the fraternity house my right leg—my kicking leg—swelled to about twice its normal size and I was taken to the university hospital. I spent the rest of the night and most of the next day with my leg packed in ice.

And that was the end of my football career.

After our last home baseball game in 1938, Coach Roettger introduced me to Harold Irelan, a scout for the Cleveland Indians. I was excited when he suggested I might have a future in professional baseball. It was something I'd always wanted from the days my father hit me grounders in the school yard at home.

First, he wanted to know if I had made any commitments to any other team.

I had worked out with the Cubs and Charlie Grimm, then the vice president and general manager, and their owner, Mr. Philip Wrigley, offered me a minor league contract. But when I told them I was still in college and wanted to continue, they understood.

Grimm said I was smart to get a college degree, which showed real class on his part, and told me to come back when I was ready to go into pro baseball. But after Irelan told me the Indians were interested, I didn't go back to see Grimm.

I also attended a White Sox tryout camp but they didn't show any interest in me.

Once I made it clear to Irelan that nobody had any strings on me, he followed me in the games I played with my amateur team that summer. He also spent a lot of time talking with my mother about my signing with Cleveland.

I liked the attention and was eager for a chance to play professional baseball. But I didn't want to do anything that might jeopardize my college eligibility at Illinois.

Irelan said, "You don't have to sign anything, just promise that you'll come to Cleveland when your college eligibility is used up."

That sounded okay to me and, with my promise, the Indians gave my parents $1,000, $500 for my mother and stepfather, and $500 for my father. They also arranged to send my mother $100 a month until I graduated, to help me get through school.

Sure, it was a verbal agreement, a verbal contract, as I realized later. But I thought as long as I didn't actually sign anything, or get any money myself, it would be okay. I was young and naive. Besides, I knew my father could use the $500.

The trouble is, my stepfather wanted the entire $1,000. I said no, that my dad deserved half because of all he'd done for me.

So my stepfather, without telling any of us, wrote a letter to Major John L. Griffith, then the commissioner of the Big Ten, telling him the arrangement we had with the Indians.

It was a pretty nasty thing to do. My stepfather was jealous of my natural father, though it was the money he wanted, not my affection. We never got along very well because I was always either outside playing a game or practicing when he thought I should be doing more work around the house.

Major Griffith sent my stepfather's letter to the athletic board at the University of Illinois to investigate and rule on my eligibility. Three of the seven members voted that I should be declared ineligible, and three voted that I should be allowed to retain my eligibility as long as my parents returned the money to the Indians. The seventh member of the board, Wendell Wilson, the athletic director, abstained.

That threw the decision into the lap of the Big Ten athletic directors who, naturally, didn't want me to compete against their schools. They declared me ineligible for the first semester of my senior year. They ruled that, if I remained an amateur during that semester, I'd regain my eligibility for the rest of my senior year.

Mr. C. C. Slapnicka, then the general manager of the Indians, offered to help, to make amends for what happened because they had given my parents money. He sent a telegram to the Big Ten stating that the Indians would renounce all claims on my services, that they would sever their relationship with me.

But it was to no avail. The ruling stood.

I resented what had happened and why it happened. I was especially resentful toward my stepfather, but not the Indians. I felt they meant well, and their offer to renounce their claim on my services was a great gesture.

But still, I was very disappointed to lose my eligibility. My initial reaction was to quit school, but my fraternity brothers convinced me to stay. I've always been thankful that I did.

I could have gone out and sold my services to the highest bidder, but I didn't feel that would be the right thing to do. There was more loyalty in those days and, besides, I was afraid it would be a black mark against me if I did something like that.

I also turned down a couple of opportunities to earn money because of the chance that I could regain my eligibility in the second semester of my senior year.

One was a chance to appear in a basketball movie with the great Hank Luisetti, called "Campus Confessions." Luisetti is the man who introduced the one-handed jump shot and wanted me because I was a great dribbler and used the two-handed set shot, as did everybody in those days.

I was to play the role of a youngster, a good basketball player, whose dad was principal of the boy's high school. The kid got into trouble and wasn't going to be allowed by his father to play on the school team. Luisetti was supposed to come along and stand up for me.

The Champaign Elks, a great semi-pro basketball team of that era, also offered me $150 a game to tour with them, but I turned them down, too. I absolutely did not want to do anything wrong because I wanted—really *expected*—to regain my college eligibility.

But then the Big Ten issued a new ruling, stating it had discovered new evidence regarding my status.

To this day, I don't know who sent it, or why. I can only suspect that it was my stepfather again, though I never asked him and he never admitted doing it.

The Big Ten claimed I had not told the whole truth about my agreement with Cleveland. There was an additional $2,200 that would be paid to me down the line, whenever—or if—I proved I was good enough to play thirty days in the major leagues with the Indians. That was the only money I was to receive, and it was my understanding, based on what Harold Irelan told me, that until I actually got the money, my eligibility would not be jeopardized.

But it was and I was devastated. I'd had my heart set on playing my final season of both basketball and baseball at Illinois where I'd been treated so well from the moment I stepped foot on the campus three years earlier.

My case became a *cause celebre* in Chicago. I'm proud to say that three nationally known sports columnists supported me in print. Jim Enright, John Carmichael, and Wendell Smith all wrote that the Big Ten was wrong, hypocritical in declaring me ineligible. But that did not help, either.

While I blamed my stepfather, I also realized later that I should not have made that verbal agreement with the Indians. It's just that I was flattered to be promised a chance to play professional baseball, and anxious to help my parents. The Depression was still on and money was very tight in those days. It seemed like those things should have been taken into consideration by the Big Ten.

After I was ruled permanently ineligible, I accepted an offer to play professional basketball with the Caesar's All-Americans of Hammond, Indiana. They were then a member of the National Basketball League, which was the forerunner of the National Basketball Association.

I was pretty good, though I wasn't very tall, and I probably could have continued to play in that league for a few years. But the Indians asked me to give up basketball and concentrate on baseball, which I was more than willing to do.

My revised plan was to play pro ball in the spring and summer of 1938 and 1939, and to return to Illinois in September each of those years to complete my education and get my degree, which was still very important to me.

It also brought me face-to-face with yet another major challenge, one that I was anxious to face.

Moving Up

When C. C. Slapnicka offered to renounce the Indians' claim on my services and sever their relationship with me in order to help me regain my college eligibility, it meant I would have been a free agent and could sign a contract with any professional baseball team.

Legally I would have been a free agent. But not morally. Not in my mind.

I would have had plenty of bargaining power because my case had generated so much publicity. A lot of sports fans in Chicago were critical of the Big Ten for making me ineligible, which was nice to know, though it didn't change my status. I was still ineligible to play varsity sports at Illinois because the Indians gave my parents money in exchange for my verbal promise to play for them.

Regardless of whose fault it was, whether I was to blame or the Indians, I still felt a strong loyalty to them which I never regretted the rest of my career. The organization treated me well, from the time Harold Irelan first talked to me, until the day I left the Indians in 1950. And the Cleveland fans were especially good to me, which I'll always remember.

After I finished my class work at Illinois in the spring of 1938 and signed a contract to officially become a member of the Indians, they assigned me to Springfield, Missouri, a team in the Class C Western Association.

I was happy to be there and eager to play, to prove myself, but I sat on the bench for a week without getting into a game. I couldn't understand why. From what I saw of the team and the league, I was satisfied I was good enough to play, though I was reluctant to ask because I didn't want to complain. But it was a week lost in my life and I was totally confused.

Finally, I asked the manager, a man named Clay Hopper, why I wasn't playing, if I'd done something wrong that I didn't know about.

Hopper told me it had nothing to do with my ability, that he was under orders to not play me until my status was clarified.

Judge Kenesaw Landis, then the commissioner of baseball, ruled that anyone who had played in the Big Ten could not be assigned to a minor league whose classification was lower than Class B. It meant that I had to be re-assigned to a higher league.

I went home for a couple of days, and then the Indians sent me to Cedar Rapids, Iowa, in the Class B Three-I League. It pleased me because I expected to start playing and also because Cedar Rapids was closer to Harvey, Illinois, than it was to Springfield, Missouri.

But first things first.

Before I reported to Cedar Rapids, Della and I got married. The date was June 5. We eloped because I was under 21 and my mother was opposed to the wedding. She thought we were too young, that we should wait. But we didn't want to, and Della's parents, Alice and Harry DeRuiter, did not object.

Tom Nesbit, a good friend from high school, was my best man. We went to a Justice of the Peace in Wheeler, Indiana, where parental permission wasn't necessary for anyone over 18.

After the ceremony we got in the car and drove to Cedar Rapids. It began a baseball career that, 10 years later, would reach the pinnacle of success, winning the World Series, and be culminated in 1970 with the greatest honor any player could hope to achieve, election to the Hall of Fame.

Cedar Rapids was a pretty good team, and so was the Three-I League, which had franchises in Indiana, Illinois, and Iowa. I'd be less than honest if I didn't admit I felt some apprehension when I reported to Cedar Rapids because I really didn't know what I was getting into. I knew I was good enough to play at Springfield, but that was Class C ball. This was a notch higher and I worried about getting in over my head.

Our manager was a veteran baseball man named Cap Crossley, who'd played a lot of minor league baseball, though he never made it to the majors. He put me in the lineup right away and I got off to a pretty good start, which helped my confidence. Della being there helped, too. We got along fine on the money I was making, all of $250 a month, which was pretty good in those days. The fans took to me and I was happy, though I didn't like the road trips.

We traveled in an old rickety bus that was driven by the coach, and some of our trips were 250, 300 miles. A lot of times, when it was a cold night, the only heat we got was from the exhaust pipe that ran down the center of the bus. But if you weren't careful when you fell asleep, you might burn your leg on the pipe.

I was the regular third baseman, but when our catcher got hit with a foul tip one night and broke a finger, I went behind the plate for a couple of games. I told Crossley I had done some catching as a kid and was willing to fill in until we got somebody else. I did okay, but nobody suggested I switch back to catching— and only once the rest of my career, when I was managing the Indians, did I go behind the plate again.

I hit .290 in 60 games with three homers and 29 runs batted in, which wasn't bad for a rookie, though the team finished sixth with a 56-63 record, 18 1/2 games behind Evansville, which won the championship.

When the Three-I season ended on Labor Day, the Indians recalled me. It was a pleasant surprise for a kid who had less than one full season in professional baseball. This time I really was apprehensive, but I was very happy to get the chance to see what the big leaguers were like up close.

Oscar Vitt was the manager of the Indians and talked briefly with me when I reported to the team. He didn't say anything special, just welcomed me, but didn't say if I'd play any or just sit on the bench and observe. It was Vitt's first year as manager of the Indians, and he had some good hitters in Hal Trosky, Ken Keltner, Jeff Heath, and Earl Averill. The pitching staff included a young fellow named Bob Feller, along with veterans Mel Harder, Johnny Allen, and Willis Hudlin.

No sooner did I join them on September 8 than I embarrassed myself and became the butt of some good-natured teasing. While warming up for infield practice with Ray Mack, another rookie who had just been called up by the Indians, I made a wild throw that hit Julius Solters, a veteran outfielder, in the head.

I always practiced getting rid of the ball quickly, which is what I was doing that day. I didn't have a good grip on the ball when I threw it, and it went over Mack's head. Naturally, Solters wasn't happy about getting hit by a rookie's wild throw, and he didn't play that day. But later he was okay.

With one exception, which I'd just as soon forget, I sat on the bench the entire four weeks I spent with the Indians.

My second day on the team Vitt put me in at third base to give Keltner a rest. It was the sixth inning of a game we were losing to Detroit, 10-2, at League Park.

Tommy Bridges was pitching for the Tigers and I can still honestly say I never saw a better curveball than a couple he threw that day. I thought they would hit me, then they broke over the plate for strikes. I walked in the seventh inning and—I think it's accurate to say —I was fortunate to ground out in the ninth. The final score was 11-3.

It was not an auspicious major league debut for the rookie third baseman from Illinois, though I'm sure it was to my dad. He was terminally ill with a brain tumor and never saw me play for the Indians, though I'll always be grateful he lived long enough to know that I made it to the major leagues. More than any other person, he's the one who got me there.

Something else that I well remember from that final month with the Indians took place in the opener of a doubleheader on the last day of the season, October 2. Detroit was in town and Hank Greenberg needed two home runs to equal Babe Ruth's then-record of 60 in one season.

The appearance of Greenberg was the main attraction for the 27,000 fans in the stadium that day. Neither the Indians nor Tigers had any place to go in the standings. New York had clinched the pennant, and Cleveland was locked in third place and finished with an 86-66 record, 13 games behind the Yankees and three ahead of the fourth-place Tigers.

Feller struck out 18 batters to break by one the major league record held by Dizzy Dean.

Somebody else who never forgot that game was an outfielder named Chet Laabs. He struck out five times.

Greenberg went down swinging twice in four trips to the plate. Though he drove in a run with a double, he didn't hit any homers in either that game or the nightcap of the doubleheader, which the Tigers also won.

Though I didn't play behind Feller that day, I could tell how hard he was throwing. He was outstanding, overpowering. I think he threw only about 10 curveballs; all the rest were fastballs.

I saw a lot of Feller in subsequent years but I don't think he ever had a better fastball than he did that day.

Something else I've got to say. I never saw Walter Johnson or any of the other old-time fireballers, but I have seen the modern strikeout pitchers and I don't think anybody ever had, or will have, a better fastball than Feller. It's a shame he couldn't have been timed with the modern radar guns they use today.

The irony of Feller's performance was that the Tigers won the game, 4-1, behind a pitcher named Harry Eisenstat, who came to us the following season. Harry was a pretty good pitcher, but he often said that game was his only claim to fame.

Everybody always talked about Feller's control problems, but I'll tell you, they weren't nearly as bad as he wanted batters to think. He'd knock guys down intentionally, though they all thought it was accidental, and nobody ever dug in on Feller, including Greenberg, who had a habit of playing policeman when he stepped into the batter's box.

Greenberg would stand there and hold his left arm up like a cop stopping traffic until he was good and ready to hit. Every pitcher hated it, but Feller was one of the few who would do anything about it. When Greenberg finally would be ready to hit, Feller would throw his fastball up and in and Greenberg would go down. Once, I remember, he knocked Greenberg down twice in a row, and I'm sure that both of those pitches were not accidental.

I got to know Feller well over the years and always respected him as a pitcher and a good friend. When I was managing the Indians, I used to tell my young pitchers, "If you want to be successful in this game, pay attention to the way Bob Feller keeps himself in shape." Nobody worked harder than Bob, before and during a game.

But I must confess, there was something about Feller that bothered me, especially when I was his manager.

He flew his own plane, which was okay as long as I wasn't with him. Once was enough.

It was 1940 and we were in Chicago, with an open date the next day. I stayed over to visit with Della's family and I accepted Feller's offer to fly back to Cleveland with him. We climbed into

his little single-engine plane, buckled up, and he taxied to the end
of the runway, getting ready to take off.

He handed me a list of about twenty-five things to do and told
me to read them off. As I did, he'd check this and that, push this
switch and that one, and finally I said to him, "Wait a minute. If
you don't know what to do without somebody reading the
directions, let me out of here."

Feller laughed and explained it was just a safety precaution.
We took off and it was a good flight back to Cleveland, but I never
flew with him again—and I used to worry everytime he went up.

After Feller set the strikeout record against the Tigers, we also
lost the second game of that season-ending doubleheader, and I
wasted no time leaving the clubhouse to get home to Della and
the University of Illinois to begin the fall semester of my senior
year.

I went back and played some games with the Hammond
team in the National Basketball League. I didn't have to worry
anymore about losing my amateur status because it was already
gone. I picked up a few dollars, and it also helped me stay in
shape for baseball as I would be going to spring training with the
Indians in late February.

Our first child, Barbara, was born on George Washington's
birthday, February 22, but she and I didn't have time to get to
know each other. A week later I left for training camp in New
Orleans, where Oscar Vitt was to give me some advice that would
have a great impact on my career.

After practice one day he called me aside and said, "Youngster, you have a great pair of hands, but you will never make it
with the Cleveland Indians as a third baseman because we've got
what I think is the greatest in Ken Keltner. I would advise you to
switch positions. Your chance of getting up here will be much
better if you play shortstop."

Vitt wasn't the best-liked man who ever managed a major
league team, nor would anybody claim that he was the smartest.

But his advice that day proved to be very good, even though
it was unusual.

In most cases it is the other way around. That is, a guy is
switched from shortstop to third base, not third base to shortstop.
I wasn't fast, but I had quick moves from playing basketball.
And, as Vitt said, I also had good hands.

I wasn't sure I wanted to switch from third base because I was worried that my weak ankles might not hold up at shortstop, where you have to move a lot more in several different directions. At third, you have to move to your left, but that's really all.

But I went along with Vitt's suggestion; after all, he was the manager, and I also could see that Keltner was entrenched at third. He was only 22 and obviously had a long and bright future.

Lyn Lary had been the Indians' shortstop in 1938, but they sold him to Brooklyn and gave the job to a rookie named Jimmy "Skeeter" Webb, whose father-in-law was Steve O'Neill.

O'Neill managed the Indians from the second half of 1935, when he replaced Walter Johnson, through 1937. Then O'Neill was replaced by Vitt in 1938 and took over as manager of Buffalo, then Cleveland's top minor league club in the Class AAA International League.

And when spring training ended, it was off to Buffalo for me, to learn to play shortstop—and ultimately take the job held by O'Neill's son-in-law, Webb, who was then the Indians shortstop.

Buffalo's shortstop was a veteran minor leaguer named Greg Mulleavy, who'd played in 77 games with the Chicago White Sox in 1930, one game for the White Sox in 1932 and one game with Boston in 1933, but never got another chance in the major leagues.

Even though it would cause Mulleavy to lose his job, he took me under his wing and taught me the fundamentals of playing shortstop, especially how to position myself behind certain pitchers and against certain hitters. Before the season ended Mulleavy retired and became a scout for Brooklyn. He's another man I'll always owe a debt of gratitude.

Another who helped me at Buffalo was Ray Mack, though we really helped each other. Mack—his real name was Mlckovsky—had been an outstanding college football player at Case Institute of Technology in Cleveland, where he'd been nicknamed the "Case Ace." He had a great season in 1938 at Fargo, North Dakota, where he hit .378 in the Class D Northern League.

Ray was a very popular hometown boy, but in a way, he was too popular for his own good. Everybody from his grade school coach to his college coach wanted to help improve his hitting. Ray listened to everybody and tried everything, but it seemed to do nothing more than hurt him.

But it was different for Mack—and me—in 1939 at Buffalo.

Before the season was a month old we were getting rave notices as a double-play combination. We became great friends and we both benefited tremendously from our association on and off the field.

So did the Indians.

I got off to a good start at Buffalo and was hitting .331 with 17 homers and 57 RBI in 115 games. On August 7, Mack and I were promoted to Cleveland. In the same transaction, Skeeter Webb was demoted to Buffalo to replace me and play for his father-in-law.

There was no resentment on the part of Webb and O'Neill. But the Buffalo players and fans didn't like it that the Indians took Mack and me away. The Bisons were leading the International League by a half game, and the Indians were out of the American League pennant race with a 51-47 record, in fourth place, 17 1/2 games behind New York.

Della, Barbara, and I drove to Cleveland with Ray. The Indians were playing the St. Louis Browns at the stadium that first night, but it would be stretching a point to say that Boudreau and Mack attracted a "huge" crowd for their debut.

The attendance was 16,467, but to Ray and me, it was really great. We liked to think the fans came to see us, but that wasn't entirely true. "Two Ton" Tony Galento, then a prominent heavyweight boxer who had lost a championship fight with Joe Louis about two months earlier, also had been advertised as a special guest. He clowned around in an Indians uniform before the game.

It turned out to be a great night, even though I made my first major league error when I fumbled what would have been a double play with the bases loaded in the sixth inning.

But we won, 6-5, and Gordon Cobbledick called me "the major hero of the evening" on the front page of the next morning's edition of the *Plain Dealer*.

There were many things about that game I'll never forget, especially that I got two hits, one a triple, in five times at bat and drove in a run. I also fielded five grounders cleanly, never mind the one I fumbled.

Willis Hudlin was our starting pitcher and I learned early on that he was not the easiest guy to play behind because he was such a tough competitor. Make an error behind Hudlin and he let you know he didn't like it.

It's also interesting that two fellows who played for the Browns that night—pitcher Jack Kramer and rookie second baseman Johnny Berardino, who hit a two-run homer—would figure prominently in my career down the road. But that's a story for later.

The first time I went to the plate as the Indians' leadoff batter in the first inning, I grounded out to Berardino. In the fourth, with the Browns leading, 1-0, I tripled to right and scored on a wild pitch. In the fifth, after St. Louis had gone ahead again, 3-2, I hit the ball hard, but lined it directly to third baseman Harland Clift.

The Browns took a 5-2 lead in the sixth inning on Berardino's homer, but I singled to center in the seventh, scoring Odell "Bad News" Hale with our third run, and we won the game with three runs in the eighth. I made the last out with a tapper back to Kramer.

Mack went hitless but drove in the winning run on a force play in the eighth, and made a couple of outstanding plays in the field.

I was interviewed after the game and still remember how nervous I was. I explained that I made the error because I was so anxious to start a double play, that I tried to throw the ball before I had a grip on it, and that I was so glad the run I let in didn't prove costly.

I also remember telling the writers that, while I didn't want to appear cocky, I thought I could make the grade with the Indians. I said I wasn't worried about my fielding, though I admitted I had been a little scared about not being able to hit big league pitching —and that's exactly the way they quoted me in the papers the next day.

After that the fans really took to Ray and me, even though it meant that two favorites were benched, Odell "Bad News" Hale, who had been playing second base, and Oscar Grimes, a very good utilityman who backed up Skeeter Webb.

I was the shortstop in all but three of the Indians' games the rest of the 1939 season, 53 in all, and batted .258 with 19 RBI.

Equally important was that the Indians played well—*better*, really—after Ray and I joined them from Buffalo. In those 56 games after our promotion on August 7 the Indians went 36-20, 16 games over .500. They were four over .500 before we came up.

Only the death of my father marred my first year in the major leagues. He underwent surgery for the brain tumor in early

September and was alert and able to hear the radio broadcast of my first game with the Indians against the White Sox in Comiskey Park later that month.

But only that one game because the doctors decided the excitement was too much.

After that series, and before we left Chicago, I visited my dad in the hospital in Harvey. It was the last time I saw him alive.

He told me how proud he was, that I had fulfilled the dreams he had for me when we played our special game of grounders in the school yard and he'd tell me, "Nice going, Louis, you broke another record."

I felt like I had.

The Year of
The Crybabies

Oscar Vitt's words were music to my ears when I returned to the University of Illinois to continue work on my degree after the 1939 season.

Before I left Cleveland he told me, "Young man, you're my shortstop next year, and it's going to be a good year." I couldn't wait for spring training to begin.

I agreed when Vitt predicted that 1940 would be a good year for the Cleveland Indians. We had a lot of positives: good hitting, good pitching, and solid defense. It was a team that had improved every year since 1936, when the Indians fell to fifth place with an 80-74 record. They won 83 games and were fourth in 1937, and climbed to third with 86 victories in 1938, the year Vitt replaced Steve O'Neill as manager.

And we finished third again in 1939 with an 87-67 record after Ray Mack and I joined the team in August of 1939.

Though the New York Yankees were perennial favorites in those years—they'd won the American League pennant and World Series four straight seasons, from 1936 through 1939—the Detroit Tigers and Boston Red Sox also were coming teams.

A lot of the so-called experts also gave us an outside chance to win a pennant for Cleveland for the first time since 1920.

They were right, though we proved them wrong. It turned out to be a terrible year.

When I reported to Ft. Myers, Florida, for spring training I felt good about our chances. And in retrospect I can say without equivocation that we should have won the pennant. I'm positive we were the best team in the league.

Jeff Heath, Ben Chapman, and Roy Weatherly were in the outfield, with Hal Trosky and Ken Keltner at the corners of the infield, and Ray Mack and I were in the middle at second base and shortstop. Rollie Hemsley and Frank Pytlak did the catching; and Bob Feller, who'd won twenty-four games and lost only nine in 1939, anchored a pitching staff that included Johnny Allen, Mel Harder, Al Smith, and Al Milnar.

Of course, also in retrospect, I realize if we had won the pennant in 1940, I probably would not have become the manager of the Indians in 1942. Oscar Vitt would've kept the job.

But even though our failure to win in 1940 helped open the door to my managerial career, I look back at that season with great regret. It represents one of the big disappointments of my career—of my life, really.

The season began sensationally as Feller pitched the first and only Opening Day no-hitter, a 1-0 victory over the White Sox in Chicago on April 16. But it quickly degenerated into the most turbulent season in Cleveland baseball history, one of the worst ever in the game.

It was the year of the "Vitt Rebellion."

It also was the year of the "Cleveland Crybabies."

The blame was directed at Vitt, who basically was a knowledgeable baseball man, but whose temperament and personality set him apart from most of the players. You never were sure where you stood with Vitt. He was upbeat and inspirational to your face, but mean and spiteful behind your back.

Vitt had been a very successful minor league manager. In 1937, he managed the famous Newark Bears, who ran away with the Class AAA International League pennant. The Bears were a farm club of the New York Yankees, and among the future major league stars on the team were Joe Gordon, Buddy Rosar, Charlie Keller, Atley Donald, George McQuinn, Willard Hershberger, Joe Beggs, and Babe Dahlgren.

A lot of people called the Bears the second best team in Organized Baseball—better than all the other 15 major league teams, except the Yankees.

With the kind of talent he had at Newark, it was easy for Vitt. He was called a "push-button manager," but it was different when he came to Cleveland. We had some good players, but not enough, and Vitt had to do more than just push buttons.

He couldn't understand why we couldn't play as well as his Newark team did, and his lack of understanding made him a poor manager.

But still, in my mind—then and now—that did not justify the action we took.

I say "we," even though Ray Mack and I, being rookies, were spared having to participate in the unprecedented action taken against Vitt by virtually all the other members of the team. Two others, Clarence "Soup" Campbell, an outfielder, and Mike Naymick, a pitcher, also were left out because they, too, were rookies.

On the morning of June 13, the same day the Nazis captured Paris in World War II, a group of ten veteran players called on Indians' owner Alva Bradley in his offices in the Marion Building, up the street from Cleveland Stadium.

They told Bradley we couldn't win the pennant as long as Vitt remained the manager.

We'd returned the night before from Boston, where we'd lost a third straight game, this one, 9-5, after leading, 5-3, going into the eighth inning. The Red Sox tied the score against Al Milnar, and won it after Vitt brought Mel Harder into the game in relief. The loss was very upsetting and so was what happened after the game.

As Harder came off the field and entered the dugout, Vitt sneered in front of the other players and said to Harder, "It's about time you won one, the money you're making."

It was embarrassing to all of us, especially Harder, a soft-spoken, well-liked man. He replied, "I gave you the best I had."

Those three straight losses to the Red Sox dropped us into third place, behind both Boston and Detroit, after we had climbed into first place on June 8.

To this day I'm not sure how or when the so-called rebellion actually started. I couldn't say who the leader was —or even if there was any one fellow who did the leading —although the most outspoken critics of Vitt were Hal Trosky, Ben Chapman and Rollie Hemsley.

Harder, the "dean" of the team, and Johnny Allen, another veteran whose opinion was highly respected, were in agreement with others in their opposition to Vitt, but constantly cautioned against doing anything rash.

Harder and Allen volunteered to call on Bradley themselves, just the two of them, but their offer was rejected.

The plan to meet with Bradley probably was formulated the first day we were in Boston, June 10. Our game was rained out that afternoon and we had time on our hands around the hotel. The way it was told to me, somebody suggested that we try to get rid of Vitt when we got back to Cleveland, but Trosky said, "Let's wait and see what happens."

What happened the next day was that we lost behind Feller, 9-2. It dropped his record to 8-4, and ours to 28-20.

In the third inning, when Ted Williams tripled and Joe Cronin homered as the Red Sox were scoring three runs, Vitt raged up and down the dugout, saying about Feller, "Look at him! He's supposed to be my ace! I'm supposed to win a pennant with that kind of pitching!"

Vitt's outburst behind Feller's back probably was the last straw. Several veteran players got together the next morning. They decided to confront Bradley and tell him they thought the only way we could win the pennant was with a new manager.

Had I been asked my opinion, or if I had not been so new on the team, I would have urged them to either wait until the end of the season, or to meet with Vitt himself, not Bradley, and try to settle the problem. Though we were struggling at the time, we were too good a team to not overcome the trouble we were experiencing on the field and in the dugout.

But I wasn't asked, I didn't volunteer, and the veterans did what they felt they had to do.

Luke Sewell, then one of Vitt's coaches, was the choice of some to take over the team, but it never reached the stage of anybody actually being considered.

It also was after that meeting in the Kenmore Hotel in Boston, and before our loss to the Red Sox the afternoon of June 12, that one of the players told Cobbledick of the plan, giving him his "scoop."

Nobody ever admitted to being the leak, and Cobby never revealed his source, though it was speculated that it was Hemsley because he wanted Vitt's job.

It was on the train back to Cleveland, after we lost the next day, that Mack and I were told what was going on, what they were planning to do.

Chapman and Hemsley called us into the men's room and said that a delegation of players led by Trosky would call on Bradley in the morning and ask him to replace Vitt. They weren't going to recommend a new manager, just that Vitt be fired.

Chapman told Mack and me that we were being left out of it because we were rookies. He said we were just starting out and that our careers could be ruined if the plan backfired. It was a considerate gesture on their part.

In addition to Campbell and Naymick, two others also were left out, Beau Bell, an outfielder, and Al Smith, a pitcher, because they also were newcomers on the team.

Trosky, who was to have led the delegation, arrived back in Cleveland to learn that his mother had died the night before, and immediately took a plane home to Norway, Iowa.

Harder took over as the spokesman in the meeting with Bradley who, I was told, listened without making a commitment. All he said to the players was that he'd look into the matter, "investigate it thoroughly and determine if any action should be taken."

None was.

Bradley also made a comment that hit home to all of us—especially later.

"If this story ever gets out," he told us, "you'll be ridiculed the rest of your lives."

That happened the very next day when Cobbledick published it on the front page of the *Plain Dealer*. It got a bigger play than the Nazis' march into Paris.

It also was right on the mark, almost as though Cobbledick had attended the meeting himself.

Bradley also proved to be right, though his prediction was somewhat exaggerated. We were ridiculed unmercifully, and if not for the rest of our lives, then certainly for the rest of that season.

Vitt did his best to shrug off the protest. He told us in a clubhouse meeting before our next game, "I see we've chased the war off page one. I'm sorry about the unfortunate thing that has happened, but I've talked the situation over with the big boss and he told me I'm remaining in charge and he's investigating the complaint which some of you made."

Vitt tried to change. He tried to get along better with everybody and was more careful about his criticism of players behind their back. But it was too late. I don't think it had any effect on anybody.

Bradley also tried to soothe the trouble. He met with us in the clubhouse a few days later. He told us that no matter how we felt about Vitt, we had to go on, that there could be no action taken then.

Bradley also asked all of us to sign a statement withdrawing our charges, our protest against Vitt. He said it wouldn't mean the matter was *completely* closed, but it would be for the rest of that season.

The statement said: "We the undersigned publicly declare to withdraw all statements referring to the resignation of Oscar Vitt. We feel this action is for the betterment of the Cleveland Baseball Club."

Twenty-one players signed it, including those who were strongest in their determination to overthrow Vitt—Hal Trosky, Ben Chapman, Rollie Hemsley—though I doubt that all of them, even *most* of them, thought it solved the problem. Mel Harder and Johnny Allen also were among those whose names were at the bottom of the statement, and so were Ray Mack and I.

Prominent among those who refused to go along with the "withdrawal" of charges against Vitt was Roy Weatherly, who in fact walked out before the meeting was ended.

Also missing were the signatures of Jeff Heath and Hank Helf, the latter an emergency catcher who had been called up from the minors a few days earlier.

The fourth player whose name did not appear below the statement was Oscar Grimes, who was out with an injury sustained when he was hit in the face with a line drive by Odell Hale during batting practice and suffered multiple fractures to his left cheek.

The statement was subsequently printed on June 17 in the three papers published in Cleveland in those days, the *Plain Dealer*, *Press*, and *News*.

But if our withdrawal statement did anything to ease the tension between us and Vitt, which is debatable, it did nothing to change the abuse we took from opponents, fans, and the media because of our so-called rebellion.

We were called "crybabies," and fans taunted us with huge wooden lollipops and baby bottles, and waved diapers at us. They pelted us on the field with fruit and vegetables—*rotten fruit and vegetables*—and many games had to be stopped to allow groundskeepers to clear the debris off the field.

Once in Detroit a couple of fans got on the field before batting practice, strung up a laundry line in front of our dugout, and hung baby clothes on it.

All of that stuff bothered us, if not consciously, then *subconsciously*, and I'm convinced the distractions—if not Vitt's arrogance and obstinance—ultimately cost us the pennant.

We weren't wrong in our criticism of Vitt. He made it very difficult to play for him. But it was wrong the way the situation was handled.

I'll say it again. We should have gone to the manager with our complaints, or waited until the end of the season. We should have told Vitt and hoped he would change, for his sake as well as ours.

Though I hadn't joined the Indians until the previous August, I knew there were problems between Vitt and the players. Once during the 1939 season, I was told, Jeff Heath and Johnny Broaca staged a fight in the dugout. The plan, which didn't work, was for Heath to throw a wild punch at Broaca that would hit Vitt.

Players don't have to love their manager to play well, or for the team to win, but two-way respect is necessary for a manager to be effective, and for a team to be successful.

We lacked that two-way respect in 1940, and because we did, the best team did not win the American League pennant that season.

Despite the sensational start that Feller gave us with the first of his three career no-hitters, 1940 began poorly in spring training. Maybe it was an omen.

I broke my ankle the third week of spring training, and we lost a promising young rookie outfielder, Paul O'Dea, who'd hit .342 in the Western Association in 1939. O'Dea was expected to have a bright future with the Indians.

Late in spring training O'Dea was hit in the right eye with a batted ball during practice. It was a freak accident; he was waiting at the batting cage for his turn to hit and leaned around the protective screen to pick up a ball that had been fouled off. At that exact moment the batter, another rookie named Lou Kahn, swung at a pitch and hit Paul squarely in the eye with the ball.

O'Dea was blinded in that eye, didn't play the rest of the season, and though he tried to make a comeback in the minor leagues—and even earned another trial with us in 1944 and 1945 when a lot of players were in the service—he was never the same and had to retire.

Fortunately I was ready by the time the season started, and played the opener. I went hitless in three trips against the White Sox' Bill Dietrich and was really nervous the last couple of innings for fear I'd be unable to make a play, and that it might cost Feller the no-hitter.

As it turned out, I fielded a grounder by Julius Solters for the second out in the ninth inning, and Ray Mack made an outstanding play to rob Taft Wright of what would have been a hit to end the game. Mack went far to his left to knock down Wright's sharp grounder and, while on his knees, threw to Trosky at first base for the final out.

The only run of the game came on Heath's single and Hemsley's two-out triple in the fourth inning.

Feller's no-hitter got us off on a roll and it seemed to be the start of something very good. But it didn't last long.

We won five of our first six games and were in or around first place through the month of April. By mid-June, when our trouble with Vitt flared up, Milnar had won eight of his first nine decisions and we'd put together an eight-game winning streak.

By late June, Feller's record was up to 12-4, Milnar's to 11-3, and on June 26 we were in first place by two-and-a-half games over Detroit and four over Boston.

But then the roller-coaster ride began.

We frittered away the lead, losing three straight, and on the Fourth of July in Detroit, where the fans were most abusive, we split a doubleheader. The Tigers won the opener, 5-3, to take over first place, then we regained the lead by winning the second game, 2-1.

It was during the doubleheader that another incident occurred that once again proved that all was not right between Vitt and his players despite the appearance of harmony that Bradley tried to create.

Joe Dobson, a spot starter, was tagged for a two-run homer by Rudy York in the eighth inning of the opener. It gave the Tigers a 5-2 lead. Vitt went to the mound and after a discussion with Dobson that seemed to last five minutes, finally waved to the bullpen for Johnny Allen.

But that quickly, Trosky rushed to Vitt's side and argued that Allen should be saved for the second game. Vitt reluctantly agreed with Trosky and canceled his call to Allen, who was not the easiest guy to get along with even when things were going well. He was very unhappy about Vitt's change of mind and made sure that everyone knew it.

That incident helped spawn rumors around the league that Trosky actually was the untitled manager of the team. There also was talk that Trosky and a couple other veterans had some secret signals amongst themselves that they used in key situations without Vitt's knowledge.

I don't think those stories were true. At least not to my knowledge. Trosky, a veteran, was the captain of the team and highly respected by all the players. But the unofficial manager who flashed secret signals? No.

But the speculation itself was troublesome and served to further compound an already difficult situation.

At mid-season I was picked on the All-Star team along with five teammates—Bob Feller, Al Milnar, Rollie Hemsley, Ray Mack and Ken Keltner. It was the first of seven times I'd be chosen, and each time was an honor. I played two innings, though I didn't get a chance to bat and we lost, 4-0, in St. Louis.

Then it was back to the business of trying to catch the Tigers, who led us by a half game—though neither of us fought a very good fight.

We lost six straight after the All-Star game but managed to stay within a half game of first place because the Tigers were playing just as poorly. They also lost six straight, which meant the Yankees and Red Sox were able to make up ground on both of us going into late July.

And as if we didn't have enough problems, I began having trouble with my appendix. I needed surgery but resolved to delay it until the season ended. It meant I had to be careful of what I ate.

I also tried an old country remedy that somebody, maybe it was trainer Lefty Weisman, recommended to prevent the problem from worsening. I played with a silver dollar taped to my abdomen because, I was told, it would prevent a rupture. Whether it worked or not, I was able to play through the end of the season, though there were times it was very painful—and it seemed I always was hungry.

We stayed neck-and-neck with the Tigers through the early part of August when another controversy arose, involving Vitt and Heath. It happened after Heath struck out as a pinch-hitter and was criticized by Vitt. They exchanged angry words and Vitt suspended Heath.

The next day General Manager C. C. Slapnicka interceded, got Heath to apologize, and Vitt lifted the suspension. On the surface, all seemed well. But not internally, and the incident kept the pot hot, if not boiling, between the manager and his players.

Despite the trouble, by mid-August we were playing pretty well again and pulled away from the Tigers. Once again we began to make plans for the World Series, and so did the Indians' front office. They got the city to invest $8,000 to install a new ramp at the stadium, assuming we'd be playing the Series there in another month.

But then, just when everything started to go in our favor, it suddenly turned around again. Everybody on the team, it seemed, went into a slump at the same time.

This was a roller-coaster ride to end all roller-coaster rides.

We lost six of the next 10 games and went into Detroit for a three-game series in September. The Tigers beat Feller, 7-2, in the opener, and went on to sweep the series. Not only was our lead cut to one game over Detroit, the Yankees were now in third place, only one game behind the Tigers, with us having 24 to play.

We went home to play Chicago, a team we'd beaten with ease most of the season.

But the slump continued and so did our losing streak. It reached five straight and we fell into a virtual tie with the Tigers. Our record was 75-56. Theirs was 76-57. We led by .0011 of a percentage point, and the Yankees were breathing hard on our backs, only two games back.

When we won the next day it was our first victory in eight games in September. But it didn't come easily and again raised doubts about the wisdom of Vitt's managerial strategy. He brought Feller in for two innings of relief and we beat the White Sox, 5-4. It raised Feller's record to 24-8.

But it also raised to nearly 300 the number of innings he had worked, more than he ever had before.

The next afternoon our long stay in first place—twenty-nine consecutive days since August 11—ended on September 9. The guy who played a key role in dropping us behind the Tigers, who were idle, was old friend Jimmy "Skeeter" Webb. The same Skeeter Webb whose father-in-law was Steve O'Neill, and whose shortstop position I had taken a year earlier. Webb doubled in the seventh inning and scored the game-winning run as the White Sox beat us 2-1.

Ten days later we went back to Detroit for another crucial three-game series, tied with the Tigers for first place with 85-61 records and eight games left.

It was a terrible greeting we got in Detroit as hundreds of Tiger fans were waiting for us at the train station. They were loud and abusive and it took us more than an hour to get through the crowd and into cabs to go downtown to the Book-Cadillac Hotel.

And once we got to the hotel we were met by even more fans—equally abusive—parading outside the hotel. They stayed into the night, yelling and calling us "crybabies."

But if we thought that was bad, it got still worse the next day at Briggs Stadium. Two fans had planted a couple of poles in front of our dugout, strung up a laundry line and hung diapers and rubber panties from it.

Ben Chapman, trying to make light of it and go along with the gag, put his bats in a baby carriage that had been rolled onto the field. He started to wheel them to the plate but was stopped by umpire Bill Summers.

The game was held up several times for the groundskeepers to pick up the debris the fans threw on the field.

We lost the first game, 6-5, as Vitt left himself open for criticism again. Harder started and was pitching well, going into the eighth inning with a 4-1 lead. When he walked Barney McCosky with one out and Charlie Gehringer singled, Vitt went to the mound and signaled to the bullpen for Feller. It was Feller's sixth relief assignment of the season, and in the previous seven days he had pitched 27 innings.

Feller failed miserably this time, but he wasn't blamed. Vitt was.

Feller was worn out from overwork, though he never complained. Vitt would do anything to win a game, and so would

Feller. But you can't continue to use a pitcher in relief as much as he used Feller, and still ask him to start in the regular rotation. It's okay once or twice, but not the way Vitt did with Feller that season.

In retrospect, the coaching staff—or maybe a contingent of players—should have gone to Vitt and talked to him about overworking our best pitcher. To the best of my knowledge, nobody ever did and it cost us.

After Vitt brought Feller into that game, Hank Greenberg greeted him with a single for one run, Rudy York singled for another run, and when Beau Bell fumbled the ball in right field, Greenberg scored the tying run. Pinky Higgins followed with another single and York came home with the go-ahead run.

Joe Dobson replaced Feller at that point and gave up another hit to score what proved to be the winning run. We fought back in the ninth against Al Benton as Roy Weatherly doubled with one out and I singled to cut the Tigers lead to one run. I got to third on a single by Trosky, but Bell struck out and Ken Keltner grounded out to end the game.

The loss dropped us into second place and, though we didn't realize it then, we were finished.

The Tigers beat us 6-0 the next day to take a two-game lead. Schoolboy Rowe pitched a five-hitter and the Tigers hit Milnar hard. It was our 15th loss in 26 games. We won the third game of the series, 10-5, behind Feller, though he didn't have good stuff. It cut the Tigers' lead to one with five games left.

That victory was Feller's 27th, most in the American League. He also led the league with 43 games and 320 innings pitched.

Our only hope was to win the next two games against St. Louis, and then win the pennant in a final three-game series against Detroit in Cleveland.

But we didn't. The Browns beat Harder and Harry Eisenstat on September 24, dropping us one and a half games behind the Tigers, who were idle. And the Yankees were still a factor. They won a doubleheader from Washington and were only a game behind us.

Al Milnar beat St. Louis for his 17th victory the next day, but the Tigers won a doubleheader against Washington. It gave them a two-game lead with three to play against us in Cleveland, which meant we had to sweep the series to win the pennant.

We all agreed it never should have come to this, but at least we still had a chance.

The Tigers arrived in Cleveland cocksure of themselves, believing—with good reason—that they had the upper hand.

Vitt knew we had to go with our best, Feller, in the first game, while Tigers manager Del Baker had plenty of leeway. He could pitch his ace, Bobo Newsom, whose record was 21-5, or go with Rowe, who'd beaten us a week earlier for his fifteenth victory, or save both of them and start a second-line pitcher. He had Newhouser, then a rookie, who had won nine games; Tommy Bridges, a great pitcher, though he was then on the downside of his career; Dizzy Trout; and Fred Hutchinson.

I heard later that Greenberg recommended that Newhouser or Hutchinson pitch the first game, but Baker chose to gamble. He started a rookie named Floyd Giebell, who had pitched only once since being called up ten days earlier from Buffalo, where his record was 15-16. The week before, in his only other start, Giebell beat Philadelphia, 13-2. He appeared in only nine games, all in relief, going 1-1 in September of 1939.

I still believe that Baker's decision to pitch Giebell was to concede that first game and come back in the next two with his best pitchers, Newsom and Rowe. It made sense, considering we had to win all three.

Giebell was known as a "junk-baller." He didn't throw hard and never threw consecutive pitches with the same velocity. He had a decent curveball, but his strength, if it was one, was very good control.

Our fans, more than 45,000 of them who came out for the game, tried to help by retaliating for the way we were treated in Detroit. They showered the field with rotten fruit and vegetables, and umpire Bill Summers—it seemed like he was always working one of our big games—called time in the first inning to warn the fans to behave.

They did, but not for long. In the second inning one of them dropped a basket of rubbish from the upper deck in left field. It landed on the head of Birdie Tebbetts, the Tigers' regular catcher, who was in the bullpen being rested along with Newsom and Rowe. Tebbetts was knocked out, but wasn't seriously injured.

Finally, Vitt took the microphone and pleaded with the fans to let the game continue.

It did, and we threatened first, in the third inning, when Ray Mack reached on an error with one out and Rollie Hemsley singled. But Giebell, known for his poise if not for great ability, struck out Feller and Ben Chapman.

Feller himself was shaky the first three innings but got through them okay. In the fourth, an inning I'll never forget, Feller walked Charlie Gehringer with one out. Greenberg struck out for the second out, and then it happened.

Rudy York hit a lazy fly ball—it appeared to me at shortstop to be nothing more than a routine fly ball—down the left field line. Chapman went back, and back, and back until he was up against the wall and couldn't go back any more. He leaped as high as he could.

In my mind's eye I can still see that lazy fly ball, and Chapman leaping.

The ball ticked off his glove and fell into the stands, 320 feet from the plate, barely inside the foul pole, for a two-run homer, York's thirty-third of the season.

Feller gave up only two more hits that day, but York's homer was all the Tigers needed.

We tried to fight back against Giebell, but he was pitching the game of his life, and Baker's gamble proved to be an excellent one.

Beau Bell and Ken Keltner singled with two out in our half of the fourth, but Giebell struck out Mack. Hemsley singled and Feller walked with one out in the fifth, but Giebell struck out Chapman and me with a variety of change-ups. And in the seventh, Mack nearly decapitated Giebell with a line-drive single up the middle, and Hemsley again reached, this time on an error by Gehringer. But Giebell struck out Chapman again to end the threat.

We couldn't score against Giebell in the eighth and ninth innings, and our pennant hopes were finished.

Giebell, who never won another major league game, was carried off the field by the Tigers, and rightfully so.

We trooped into our clubhouse and it was hard to believe that it was all over. Nobody said much of anything, including Vitt, while the Tigers whooped and hollered in their celebration on the other side of the Stadium.

While we were losing to the Tigers, Philadelphia was beating New York to also eliminate the Yankees. It clinched the pennant for Detroit.

We won the next two games behind Mel Harder and Al Milnar, but it didn't matter.

I guess you can say the only excitement occurred when Tebbetts, who was back in the lineup, was served a warrant for his arrest during the visitors' half of the seventh inning. It seems that Birdie beat up the guy he thought dropped the rubbish on his head the day before.

We finished second, one game behind the Tigers and one ahead of New York. It was a tremendous disappointment, one that I'll never forget because—I'll say it again—we should have won the pennant.

Personally, it was a good season. I hit .295 with nine homers and 101 runs batted in. I led American League shortstops in fielding, the first of nine seasons I would do so, and was voted the American League's rookie of the year by the Chicago Chapter of the Baseball Writers Association.

But I was sorry for all that had happened during that most turbulent season.

And especially sorry the way it ended.

Goodbye, "Ol' Oz"

My only delay in leaving Cleveland and going home to Harvey after the 1940 season was to have my appendix out. I was tired of hurting and anxious to eat regularly again. As Della always said (and still does), nothing could pain me as much as having to watch what I ate.

Along with my eagerness to have the operation, I was in a big hurry to get out of Cleveland. The fans and newspapermen wouldn't let us forget the season and what had happened. I was really tired of that, too, and didn't need to be reminded.

I was able to put it out of my mind except during the World Series between Detroit and Cincinnati. I kept thinking that we belonged there, that it should have been us, not the Tigers, who played the Reds, and I'm sure I wasn't alone in those thoughts.

Oscar Vitt's regime officially ended on October 8, the very day Cincinnati beat Detroit, 2-1, in the seventh game of the World Series. I say officially because everyone—including "Ol' Oz," as he called himself—knew it was over long before that.

Alva Bradley, who always said he hired the manager and the public fired him, announced that Vitt would not be offered a contract for 1941, and that a new manager would be named soon. Vitt left with a three-year record of 262-198. Included were two third-place finishes and one second, which wasn't bad, except—again—it should have been better.

Bradley also thought so. He was quoted as saying we should have won the 1940 pennant, and left no doubt about his opinion as to why we failed.

"Our real trouble started June 13, when a group of 10 players came to my office. They made four distinct charges against their manager and asked for his dismissal," he said in a story that appeared in the *Cleveland News*, written by Ed McAuley, who covered the Indians in the 1940s and 1950s.

Bradley said he didn't give in to the players because "It was not only a Cleveland problem, it affected baseball in general, and I felt I should do everything in my power to protect the game of baseball."

But he also admitted, "The four charges made against Vitt, on investigation I have made, were 100 percent correct."

None of it made me feel any better, and I'm sure it didn't soothe any of my teammates either.

Bradley waited more than a month before he named a new manager, and there was some speculation that it would be Luke Sewell.

Sewell would have been a popular choice. He was a very good baseball man and I think he would have been a good manager for us. Luke was quiet, unassuming, absolutely the opposite of Vitt. He was a friend to everybody, a genuinely nice guy. He had been a coach under Vitt in 1940 and, when the players asked Bradley to fire Vitt, many were hoping Sewell would be appointed to take over the team.

But during the rebellion year, Bradley never indicated—at least not publicly—that he favored anybody, though a story that came out several years later reported that he initially wanted Sewell.

Before Sewell died in 1987, a writer quoted him as saying that Bradley offered him Vitt's job three times in 1940. The story said that Bradley first approached Sewell in New York after the owner's publicized meeting with the unhappy players on June 13.

Bradley was supposed to have said to Sewell, "You've got to take it."

Sewell, who was fiercely loyal to Vitt, said he replied, "I don't have to take it . . . and what is going to happen to Oscar?"

Bradley reportedly answered, "We are going to put him in a sanitarium," to which Sewell responded, "Oh, no!"

Nobody will know for sure what happened and what actually was said because both men have since passed away.

The only comment I ever heard attributed to Bradley on the subject of Sewell was that he reportedly said in a private conversation that Luke was passed over because of a fear of public criticism, whatever that was supposed to mean.

Whatever the case, on November 12, Bradley announced the hiring of Roger Peckinpaugh to manage the Indians. Sewell would stay on as a coach, although seven weeks into the 1941 season he replaced Fred Haney as manager of the St. Louis Browns. The Browns dropped to seventh that year, but won the pennant under Sewell in 1944. He managed St. Louis for six seasons, and Cincinnati from the final three games of 1949 through mid-1952.

I've often thought about how different my career would have been if Bradley had hired Sewell instead of Peckinpaugh. Who knows? We might have done better in 1941 under Sewell than we did under Peckinpaugh and he might have remained the manager. Bradley's choice of Peckinpaugh was something of a surprise. He had previously managed Cleveland from 1928 until he was replaced by Walter Johnson in 1933. In those five-plus seasons under Peckinpaugh the Indians were never a contender, and their highest finish was third, 24 games behind Philadelphia in 1929.

"Peck," as everyone called Peckinpaugh, like Sewell, was a nice man, a man of poise and restraint. It was obvious that Bradley felt a man of his character and personality was necessary to heal the wounds we all suffered in the strife-torn 1940 season. Though I didn't know Peckinpaugh, based on what I'd heard about him, I thought he would be good for the team and I was glad he got the job.

That winter Peckinpaugh and General Manager C. C. Slapnicka made some trades that everybody thought would help us, though in retrospect, they didn't do much. Catcher Frankie Pytlak, pitcher Joe Dobson, and second baseman Odell Hale were sent to Boston for outfielder Gerry "Gee" Walker, catcher Gene Desautels, and pitcher Jim Bagby. Walker and Bagby would figure later in my career as manager of the Indians, but that's a story to be told down the road.

We also had a number of promising youngsters slated to report for spring training in Ft. Myers, Florida, among them a third baseman named Bob Lemon and a rookie catcher named Jim Hegan.

Peckinpaugh was optimistic, saying we surely would—not *could* but *would* —win the pennant.

We started well enough, winning 11 of our first 15 games. We took over first place on April 29 and stayed there until June 27, 60 days in all.

Bob Feller was pitching well again, but Al Milnar and Al Smith weren't up to what they'd done in 1940 when they won 33 games between them. And Mel Harder experienced elbow trouble that required surgery at the end of the season. He started only 10 games and won just five.

Hal Trosky, our captain and big hitter, who led the team with 25 homers in 1940, suddenly began to suffer migraine headaches. They curtailed his effectiveness, cut short his season, and eventually drove him out of baseball. He played only 89 games in 1941, hitting just 11 homers and driving in 51 runs.

And opposing pitchers early on discovered a weakness in Ray Mack, who'd hit .283 as a rookie, but never again approached that figure. He, too, soon would be out of baseball.

As for me, I also had a down season, and nobody was more disappointed than I. My average fell to .257 with 10 homers and 56 runs batted in, slightly more than half as many as I had in 1940. Don't ask me what happened, I don't know. I tried as hard, but nothing worked as well.

After falling into second place in late June we stayed close to New York for about three weeks. But then, just as we turned ice-cold, the Yankees got red-hot, and though we were still second by August 5, we were 12 games behind. It was never a race after that as we went 10-21 in August and 10-16 in September.

Despite my average dropping almost 40 points, I was pleased to be picked on the All-Star team again. I went 2-for-2 as the American League beat the Nationals, 7-5, in Detroit. Ted Williams, the best left-handed hitter I ever played against or with, hit a three-run homer in the ninth inning.

Another highlight of that otherwise disappointing season occurred the night of July 17—on my twenty-fourth birthday—at Cleveland Stadium.

This one revolved around Joe DiMaggio, the best right-handed hitter I ever played against or with. Though he was only three years older than I, DiMaggio was my idol from the time he broke in with the Yankees in 1936, when I was a freshman at the University of Illinois.

In fact, DiMaggio was the reason I wore No. 5—his number—and it pleases me that both have been retired, mine by the Indians and DiMaggio's by the Yankees.

The day before, July 16, at old League Park, DiMaggio got three hits, a double and two singles, against us in a 10-3 victory for the Yankees. The first hit came early, a first-inning single to center off Milnar.

It extended DiMaggio's consecutive-game hitting streak to an ongoing-record 56 games. But he wasn't satisfied with that first hit. He looped a single to center in the third, again off Milnar, walked and grounded out in his next two at-bats, and finished the day with a long double to the gap in left-center off Joe Krakauskas. He also scored three runs, and the 3-for-4 game raised his average to a sensational .545 for the streak.

It perfectly set the stage for what happened the next night, in front of 67,468 roaring, frenzied fans in the stadium. There had never been a larger crowd to see a major league night game. Most of them were there because of DiMaggio's streak, but the fact is, we were still in the pennant race, trailing the Yankees by two games.

It was another night I'll never forget, and not just because it was my birthday.

Al Smith, a left-hander with a good curveball and decent control, started for us, and Bagby, the pitcher we obtained from Boston during the winter, finished.

Between them—with the help of Ken Keltner—they ended DiMaggio's hitting streak. It is one of the few records in baseball that I doubt will ever be broken. And to make DiMaggio's feat even more sensational, he went on to hit safely in another 16 consecutive games after we stopped him.

Keltner literally stole two hits from DiMaggio, the first in the first inning, the second in the seventh.

Keltner played a very deep third base the entire game, figuring, as we all did, that DiMaggio wouldn't bunt as a matter of pride. Something else that worked in our favor and certainly hurt DiMaggio was that it rained before the game. Not only were the first- and third-base lines slow, so was the area around the plate. Batters, especially right-handed batters, as DiMaggio was, couldn't get a good start out of the box.

But that's not to take anything away from Keltner. In the first inning DiMaggio pulled a low-inside curve down the line at third that Keltner backhanded and, with his strong arm, nipped Joe at first by half a step.

DiMaggio walked in the fourth inning, and the fans actually booed. They cheered in the bottom of the fourth when we tied the game at 1-1 on an inside-the-park home run by Gee Walker.

Then in the seventh, when the Yankees went ahead, 2-1, DiMaggio did it again, and so did Keltner. Joe hit another shot down the line. Keltner backhanded the ball behind the bag, just as he did in the first inning, and again his throw to first was on the mark and in time.

DiMaggio batted again in the eighth after the Yankees had taken a 4-1 lead, and Smith was replaced by Bagby. This time Joe came up with the bases loaded and one out and hit Bagby's pitch toward me. The ball came out routinely, but the last instant it took a nasty hop. I threw my hands up, actually to protect my face, and caught the ball with my bare hand. I recovered in time and my throw to Ray Mack at second base started a double play that ended the inning.

That was DiMaggio's last at-bat and his streak was stopped—though we tried like the devil to get him another chance to extend it.

We almost tied the score in the bottom of the ninth, which would have sent the game into extra innings and allowed DiMaggio to bat in the tenth.

Only a base-running mistake by Larry Rosenthal, an outfielder, who tripled as a pinch hitter for Mack leading off the ninth, deprived us of a tie and DiMaggio of another at-bat.

Trosky, the next batter, hit a hot grounder to first baseman Johnny Sturm. Rosenthal started home and should have scored, but turned and went back to third when Sturm fielded the ball.

Then Clarence "Soup" Campbell, a pinch-hitter for Bagby, bounced the ball back at relief pitcher Johnny Murphy. There was no stopping Rosenthal this time and he was caught in a rundown between third and home for the second out.

Campbell compounded the blunder by sitting on first instead of taking second as Rosenthal was being run down, but it didn't really matter as Roy Weatherly grounded out to end the game.

Though nearly half the season remained, it was all downhill the rest of the way, and this time we had no excuses, no manager to blame, only ourselves.

The team that Peckinpaugh said would—not could—win the pennant, finished in a tie with Detroit for fourth place, with a 75-79 record, 26 games behind the Yankees. Boston was nine games ahead of us in second place, and Chicago two ahead in third.

I went home to Harvey and my job of coaching the Illinois freshman basketball and baseball teams.

Little did I realize that within two months Slapnicka would resign, Peckinpaugh would be promoted and my life would be drastically changed.

The
"Boy Manager"

C. C. Slapnicka's resignation as general manager of the Indians near the end of the 1941 season came as a surprise, though his health had been deteriorating for some time. Earlier in the year he'd suffered a heart attack, his second, and at his age, 54, the daily stress of baseball was too much.

"Slap," as he was nicknamed, had been Alva Bradley's right-hand man since 1935, and I'm sure our failure to win the pennant in 1940, and again in 1941, had much to do with his decision to leave the organization.

It was Slapnicka who hired Oscar Vitt, and he also was the one who highly recommended that Roger Peckinpaugh be given another chance to manage the team when Vitt was fired.

After leaving the Indians, Slapnicka went back to scouting, a job he loved and excelled in—and which demanded less of himself. Before taking over as general manager of the Indians, he had discovered Bob Feller; he also is the scout who found and signed Ken Keltner, Hal Trosky, Jeff Heath, Earl Averill, Mel Harder, Jim Hegan, and others.

Later, during Bill Veeck's ownership, Slapnicka rejoined the Indians as a scout and also was credited with finding Herb Score, who would have been one of the greatest pitchers of all time if he had not been injured.

But Slapnicka's resignation wasn't the only surprise that winter of 1941-42.

So was the promotion of Peckinpaugh from field manager to general manager—and then the hiring of that brash young guy named Lou Boudreau to manage the Indians.

My first chore after being told by Mr. Bradley that the job was mine was to meet the press. To be honest about it, I was more scared than when I was interviewed by the directors.

When I isolated myself in my hotel room on November 24, the night before I was to be introduced, I practiced answering questions I thought I'd be asked. The first one, of course, pertained to my ability to handle both jobs, managing and playing shortstop.

At the time, perhaps because of my youth and inexperience, I didn't really anticipate any problem. Looking back at it, I realize how naive I was. I'm not saying I was in over my head, but I am saying I didn't really become a good player-manager until after that first or perhaps second season.

Part of it was that, less than two weeks after I got the job, World War II began and I immediately lost Feller, the greatest pitcher in the game. He enlisted in the Navy two days after the Japanese bombed Pearl Harbor. Then Hal Trosky announced his retirement because of migraines (though he made a comeback in 1944 with the Chicago White Sox).

But none of that was on my mind that day in Cleveland, at League Park, when I was introduced to the media.

I've always considered it fortunate that there was no television in that era, and not much radio coverage either. It was a lot easier dealing with the newspaper reporters.

Television, because of its immediacy, has made such a big change in the way all sports are covered today. The newspaper guys weren't looking for sensational stories then. But now they have to come up with a different angle all the time, which often makes it as difficult for the players and managers as it is for the writers.

Television is great for the team owner because it helps promote the games and sell tickets. But it's tough on a manager, especially a player-manager, because it demands so much of his time before and after the games are played.

I'm afraid, if I were just starting out as a manager, I would not be very popular among the media. I'd limit press conferences to a certain specified amount of time, and I'd restrict the reporters' access to the clubhouse.

And I'd absolutely have a cooling-off period after every game.

A clubhouse is like a second home for the players. They should be able to say things that don't get reported. A lot of players pop off in the clubhouse. Then they're shocked to see their comments in the papers and decide they won't talk to reporters anymore—even though they're the ones who made the mistake.

It was a lot easier in my day.

I think I handled that first press conference okay.

The reporters were surprised to see me walk through the door of Mr. Bradley's private office when he said, "I want you fellows to meet the new manager of the Indians." There'd been no speculation, as there would be today, that I was even a candidate. To the best of my knowledge my name had never been mentioned and nobody ever called me to ask if I was interested.

I remember one of the writers saying, "That kid?"

Yes, that kid. I was immediately dubbed the "Boy Manager," with good reason. Until then the youngest men to manage major league baseball teams were Bucky Harris and Joe Cronin, both hired by Clark Griffith, the owner of the Washington Senators. I was three years younger than both Harris, when he was hired in 1924, and Cronin in 1933.

Mr. Bradley's introduction pleased me and made me feel more comfortable.

He said, "The more I inspected the qualifications of various other candidates, the more I became convinced that we couldn't afford not to take advantage of Lou Boudreau's natural gift of leadership. I didn't know of another man of whom I could be so certain that he would be thoroughly respected by the players, press and public. Lou is smart, he's a great ball player, a fine young man, a fighter and a leader."

Nobody could ask for a better endorsement from his boss.

Mr. Bradley also said he'd had somebody else in mind—I'm sure it was Burt Shotton, who'd managed Class AAA Columbus to the American Association pennant in 1941—but the more he thought about me, the more he thought he had a fellow who knew the Indians' situation and the players.

Not everybody spoke—or wrote—so optimistically about me.

One Cleveland reporter said in the paper the next day, "Great! The Indians get a Baby Snooks for a manager and ruin the best shortstop in baseball." That seemed to be the general consensus, that by taking over as manager of the Indians, I would not be capable of continuing as a good shortstop.

There also was a nasty editorial that appeared in a newspaper in Detroit, where baseball fans still hated the Indians from their "crybaby" days of the "Vitt Rebellion."

In part, it read: "Being made manager of that outfit after two years in the majors and having to face the irascible Cleveland public and a press box full of second guessers is enough to warrant calling out the Society for the Prevention of Cruelty to Children."

But by and large the press was pretty good to me then—and I've got to say, throughout my career. I got my share of criticism, but I had no complaints about my relationship with the media, and still don't.

George Martin, who convinced the other directors of the Indians to give me the job, was quoted as saying, "Boudreau has practically been the manager right along. Besides, he was the captain or leader of every team he ever played on. That boy's a natural."

I also was encouraged by several telegrams I received the next couple of days.

One came from Steve O'Neill, whom I'd played for at Buffalo, and who had previously managed the Indians for two and a half seasons. O'Neill said, "I knew you had the makings of a leader, but did not expect it to happen so early in your career."

Peckinpaugh wired his best wishes, too. "Get in there and pitch. You can do it," he said.

I even heard from one of the "bad boys" on the 1941 team, Roy Weatherly, who had been suspended once during the season by Peckinpaugh. "It will be a pleasure to work for you if I'm still on the club next year," Weatherly said in his telegram.

And Jeff Heath, who'd had several altercations with both Vitt and Peckinpaugh, was quoted in a newspaper as saying, "I think Boudreau will make the best manager Cleveland ever had." It was nice to read that kind of praise.

One of my first statements to the press came when I was asked if I was intimidated by what had happened to Vitt. I replied, "We'll start from scratch. I think the boys have forgotten the Vitt incident. Anyhow, I'll never ask anybody to do anything except hustle for me. And anyone who doesn't hustle won't be long with the club."

I told them I'd learned a valuable lesson from Vitt, that is, to be honest with your players, face-to-face and behind their backs. I said my office would be open to players at all times, that if any of them had a complaint or a problem with me, to settle it in my office, not in front of 10 or 15 people.

But that's not to say I didn't make any mistakes. I did. A ton of them. I was always learning.

After the press conference ended, Mr. Bradley commended me for the way I'd handled the reporters. I went home to Harvey for a few days. I was still glowing with pride and happily accepted the congratulations of Doug Mills and Wally Roettger, my two mentors. Della also was pleased, though I'm sure she still had some misgivings about my ability to handle both jobs.

Then it was off to the minor league meetings in Jacksonville, Florida, where Bradley, Peckinpaugh, and I set out to strengthen the team. We felt that with just a few additions—especially pitching—we could be right back in contention as we'd been in 1938, 1939, and 1940.

It was while we were in Florida that I officially hired Burt Shotton, who was genuinely appreciative of the opportunity to get back to the major leagues. He played 14 seasons for the St. Louis Browns, Washington, and the St. Louis Cardinals from 1909 to 1923, and managed the Philadelphia Phillies from 1928 to 1933, and Cincinnati in 1934.

I've got to say that Shotton was a loyal coach the four years (1942-45) he worked for me, though I also must say there were times I got the impression that he wasn't as happy when we won as the rest of us were. Perhaps it's because I got the job he had wanted, that he had expected to get.

The rest of the winter was very hectic. Everybody wanted to interview the "Boy Manager." While the attention was nice, it didn't leave much time for other things, like getting around and visiting my players, which would have been helpful to them and me.

But before we could make any moves to help the team, the war broke out and nobody could be sure what lay ahead. We knew players would be leaving to enter the service and we'd have to do the best we could with some fellows who weren't of major league caliber.

There even was speculation that major league baseball would be put on hold for the duration of the war, although President Roosevelt quickly assured everybody that he felt the game should continue as a way of boosting morale.

There also was speculation by some—which annoyed me very much—that I would be only a rubber stamp for Peckinpaugh, that he would still be running the Indians and, while I had the title of manager, I would be nothing more than his "captain" on the field.

I'm sure it bothered Peck, too.

But the speculation was absolutely untrue. Sure, I relied on Peckinpaugh's experience and judgment. I would have been foolish not to. After all, Peck had been in the major leagues for more than 30 years, from the time he broke in as a shortstop with the Indians in 1910. He played 17 years for the Indians, Yankees, Washington, and White Sox, and also was a coach, manager, scout, and front office executive. He was like a father and helped me a lot.

But I called the shots from the beginning. Some of my decisions were not so good, I'll admit. But I made them. I was in charge. Not Peckinpaugh.

Some of those bad decisions were made the first couple of days in spring training. But I survived them, and learned from them.

One mistake, which is embarrassing even now, more than 50 years later, was my attempt to instill a rah-rah spirit on the team. My intentions were good, but the plan was bad. I wanted the players to subordinate their personal ambitions and interests for the good of the team. I wanted them to play like we did in college.

With that in mind, the day before spring training was to begin I had signs put up around the locker room that said, "Have a will to win and a passion to score," and "He who refuses to be beat, can't be beat," things like that.

Within 24 hours of the players' arrival, the signs were torn down. Not only torn down, but tobacco juice spit all over them.

I heard that some of the players referred to me as "Joe College," behind my back, of course, and I didn't bother putting the signs back up.

It was a lesson I learned in a hurry, that major league ball players are professionals, not college boys, and while it's good to have the kind of team spirit I tried to instill, putting up those signs was not the way to do it.

My teams eventually did develop that kind of spirit, where a player would go out of his way to slide hard into second base to break up a double play, or give himself up to advance a runner, even though it did nothing to enhance his own statistics. But it didn't happen because I had put up a lot of signs in the clubhouse.

That's one of the biggest reasons—along with the advent of television—that I think it is so much more difficult to manage a major league baseball team today.

Since free agency came into the game in the mid-1970s and players are able to sell their services to the highest bidders, individual statistics are most important, not the intangible contributions a player makes to a winning team. And when a player has a multiyear contract that's guaranteed no matter what he or his team does, where is the incentive?

In my day, when a player negotiated his contract with the general manager, he could point out the times he coaxed a walk instead of swinging for a hit at a 3-and-1 pitch, or bunted on his own, or did any number of things to help the team win, not to pad his statistics.

But now, with the average major league salary being more than the entire payroll of teams in my day, and players free to jump from team to team, the numbers—batting average, home runs, runs batted in—are what matters most.

I can't blame the players for wanting to make as much money as they can, but it certainly makes it more difficult to be a major league manager today—a *successful* major league manager of a *winning* team.

My attempt to inject team spirit in my players by posting signs wasn't the only mistake I made that first spring training.

I felt it was important for the writers covering the team to do what they could to help us by not writing controversial stories, stories that might be injurious and possibly cause dissension between the players, and *among* the players and me.

It was with that in mind that I asked the regular beat reporters in my first press conference to let me know what they were writing before the stories were sent to their newspapers.

Gordon Cobbledick of the *Cleveland Plain Dealer* put me in my place in a hurry.

Cobby made it clear he hoped the team would have a good season and that I would be successful as a manager.

But he also made it clear that he and the other writers covering the team—Ed McAuley of the *Cleveland News*, and Franklin Lewis and Frank Gibbons of the *Cleveland Press*—were paid by their newspapers, not the Indians. He told me I should run the ball club and let them write the stories, which was good advice that I never forgot.

I learned something else early in spring training that opened my eyes to the job ahead of me.

The first week we were in training camp in Ft. Myers, Florida, Gerry "Gee" Walker came into my office, looked me straight in the eyes and said that he had applied for the job I got. He also told me that he could do better than I was doing, or would do that season. It was an eye-opener.

Walker was an outspoken veteran outfielder we'd acquired from Boston the year before. He was a pretty good player, a real hustler, but he was no longer a kid.

I can't say I resented him for the things he said to me that day. After all, he only did the same thing I did in applying for the job when Peckinpaugh was moved up to general manager. But I was somewhat concerned about how Walker would be that season when the going got rough, as it probably would.

We wound up selling Walker to Cincinnati that spring. It wasn't that I feared he'd cause trouble, but all things considered, he was 33 and we had some young outfielders we wanted to play. Hank Edwards and Oris Hockett were coming up from the minors, and we still had Jeff Heath, Roy Weatherly, and Clarence "Soup" Campbell.

On the other hand, I'm sure there were players who resented me, though I wouldn't let it affect the way I ran the team. We worked hard on fundamentals and I delegated authority to my coaches. They'd go to a player and say, "The kid," that was me, "wants us to do it this way." And if the player didn't like it, the coach would tell him to "go see No. 5," which also was me.

At the onset of spring training I let the players set their own rules, with my approval, of course, and one of them was that everybody had to be in his own hotel room by midnight. Violation of any rule would result in a minimum fine of 50 dollars, which was a lot of money in those days.

There were some violations, of course, which was to be expected. Anytime you put together 35 or 40 grown men away from home for a period of five or six weeks, there's bound to be one fellow or another—or more—who will go out on the town, take some liberties.

One particular Saturday night I decided to look around the bars in the neighborhood of the hotel and saw Chubby Dean sitting and drinking with a young lady. It was nearly midnight, so I reminded him about the curfew. He said, "Okay, Lou, I'm on my way."

I left and went back to the hotel, waited about a half hour in the lobby, then called Dean's room. Jim Bagby, who was Dean's roommate, answered the phone. Anyone who knew Bagby, knew he had a speech impediment.

I told him I was making a bed check, and he said, in his distinctive way, "Well, I'm here and so is my roomie, Chub."

I asked him to put Dean on the phone and Bagby said, again as only he could say it, "Aw, Lou, Chub is sleeping, he's sawing wood, I hate to wake him."

I insisted.

So, the next voice I hear was a guy with a speech impediment—Bagby, of course—saying, "Hello, Lou, this is Chubby Dean. I got back a minute or two before midnight."

I said, "Good, I'm coming up. I want to see you and Bagby about something."

When I got to the room, Bagby opened the door and said, "Aw, Lou, you know damn well Chubby's not in."

It cost Dean $200. But I let Bagby off for nothing. In fact, I even praised him in a meeting for protecting his teammate. He couldn't pull it off, though he had tried.

All in all, I was satisfied the way that first spring training went for me and the team. With the enthusiasm of youth, I was optimistic that we would have a good year, perhaps even be a pennant contender.

But it's also accurate to say I was not very realistic.

A lot of players came and went because of the war, including many who never would have warranted a second look under normal conditions.

And we didn't have Feller. He was aboard a battleship in the Navy, where he would spend 44 months during what should have been the prime of his career.

A Great Start

Opening Day always is special. The mistakes and failures of the previous season are forgotten. Everybody starts with a clean slate—and in first place. It's a great feeling.

That first game in 1942 was extra-special for me. We came out of spring training in good shape, especially our pitchers, and while nobody considered us the favorite to win the American League pennant, I felt we had a sound club and had a chance to do something.

It was a pressure year for me. Everybody was paying close attention to the "Boy Manager," the decisions I was making and how the team was doing, though I felt the fans were solidly behind me because of my playing ability.

The war was raging in Europe and the Pacific, and we were never sure from one day to the next who we might lose to the draft, or who would quit baseball to work in a defense factory for the duration. That says something about the baseball salaries at the time, although a lot of players also quit baseball to work in a factory in order to get a deferment from the draft.

The draft board classified me 4-F because of my bad ankles. I had an arthritic condition in one, and the other was just plain weak from all the basketball I had played when I was younger.

As somebody once wrote, I was the only major league baseball player who walked on the outside of his ankles. I had trouble with them all of my career and beyond, even when climbing steps to get to the press box when I went into radio after my playing and managing careers were finished.

That 1942 team had pretty good balance, at least on paper, with a pitching staff that included Jim Bagby, Mel Harder, Harry Eisenstat, Al Smith, Vernon Kennedy, and Al Milnar.

With Feller in the Navy, Bagby would be our No. 1 pitcher, though I hesitated to call him our "ace." He wasn't really my kind of a guy, though I can't put my finger on why. We had our problems, though nothing really serious. He always seemed to think that people were making fun of his speech impediment, but if they were, I didn't know about it, and I certainly wasn't among them.

Gene Desautels and rookie Otto Denning would handle our catching, and three-quarters of our prewar infield was intact, with me at shortstop, Ray Mack at second, and Ken Keltner at third.

Les Fleming, another rookie, took over at first base for the retired Hal Trosky, and our starting outfielders were veterans Roy Weatherly and Jeff Heath, and rookie Oris Hockett.

I was satisfied we could be respectable, but *how* respectable was anybody's guess. The Yankees, who'd won the pennant five of the previous six years, would be strong again, and so would Boston, though it was hard to figure the rest of the league because of the manpower situation.

One New York oddsmaker picked us for fifth, at 12-to-1 to win the pennant, and placed us behind the Yankees, Boston, Chicago and St. Louis. That was okay with me; you win on the field, not in the betting parlors, but inwardly I was a little annoyed that we weren't getting more respect.

If nothing else, we at least had rid ourselves of the reputation for turmoil and controversy that had plagued Cleveland teams the past few years. As Gordon Cobbledick wrote in the *Plain Dealer* at the end of spring training:

"In the old days . . . the Indians were a hell-raising ball club in one fashion or another and you always felt that you couldn't afford to be very far away from them.

"Some bent the elbow too freely, and some were chronically mad at somebody, and some talked too much.

"It wasn't always pleasant, but nobody could ever say it was dull.

"Now life among the Indians promises to be exceedingly pleasant and serene—and unspeakably dull. Nobody is going to get drunk and nobody is going to demand that the manager be fired, and nobody is going to do any of the things that have earned the Indians so much attention from press and public in recent years."

I thought that was pretty good. I was pleased by Cobby's assessment.

One aspect of managing that I regretted, and which I had not anticipated, was that I no longer could pal around off the field with the players. Many of them were close friends, especially Ray Mack and Ken Keltner, but I had to be careful not to show any favoritism.

I also had to be careful not to see everything that was going on off the field. As Roger Peckinpaugh told me, the things a manager doesn't see sometimes are more important than the things he does see.

It was a tough lesson for me and added to the pressure of my first season as a manager.

We came out of spring training in good shape, but the weather complicated our opening. While barnstorming north with the New York Giants, we seemed to run into rain everywhere. We couldn't play for an entire week—seven consecutive rainouts—before the opener in Detroit.

We finally got to play, and it was a great beginning.

In my first game as a major league manager, on April 14, we beat the Tigers, 5-2. I got two hits, a double and a single, but the offensive star for us was Fleming, the rookie first baseman who was filling Trosky's big shoes. Fleming homered, doubled, and singled. Bagby went eight innings for the victory.

It was the first of 1,162 games my teams would win in my 16-year managerial career and, yes, I was as proud as could be.

Bagby never wanted to be taken out of a game, but I replaced him in the ninth when the first two batters reached. Joe Heving came in and wrapped it up.

I never liked it when Bagby objected to my bringing in a reliever for him, but on the other hand, I have to give him credit for wanting to stay in the game. He always wanted the "honor"—which is what he called it—of pitching out of his own jams.

In a way, Bagby was right. A pitcher should know himself best, and how he can get a certain guy out. But I always found that too many pitchers were unwilling to admit they'd lost some of their stuff, or that they were tired, and Bagby was one of them.

My theory always was that you can never take a pitcher out too soon, only too late.

Whatever, one of the toughest jobs a manager has is knowing when to replace a pitcher. It's something I felt I never did well until after I'd managed a couple of years.

Winning the opener got us off and running, but the euphoria didn't last long.

We proceeded to lose our next three, including the home opener at the stadium, 1-0, to Chicago. It was a big disappointment to me, especially in front of nearly 25,000 fans. But I refused to let it get me down, and just that quickly it turned around again.

We beat Chicago, 1-0, on April 18 at the stadium as Bob Feller was home on leave from the Navy and provided some moral support, and we went on to win 13 consecutive games, setting an Indians franchise record that has been equaled but never broken.

After six straight the coaches got together with me and we agreed not to shave until we lost, which I hoped would motivate the players to play harder and keep everybody loose. We were all having fun and for another week Burt Shotton, with his gray whiskers, Oscar Melillo, George Susce, and I grew beards.

It was terrific, and with each victory we became bigger heroes in Cleveland.

We won four straight from the White Sox, two in St. Louis, two more in Chicago, three in Philadelphia and two in Washington. We climbed into a first-place tie with the Yankees after seven straight, and were on top all by ourselves with our ninth in a row on April 28.

I was happy, of course, although realistically I didn't think we were that good. We were getting a lot of breaks, a lot of things were being handed to us.

And just as all good things end, so did our winning streak. We lost, 8-4, in Boston on May 3—and the coaches and I shaved.

It was a disappointing defeat, not because I expected to win all the rest of our games, but because of the way we lost. We cracked wide open in the field and handed the Red Sox all their runs.

And with that, another roller-coaster ride began.

We lost six straight, won four straight and eight of nine games, then lost five more in a row, falling into fourth place by the end of May. I tried everything. Juggled the lineup. Changed the batting order. A couple of times I even had my pitcher bat seventh.

We were 17-12 in June, 16-14 in July, 10-16 in August, and 8-16 in September. We finished fourth, 28 games behind the Yankees, at 75-79, identical to our won-lost mark under Peckinpaugh in 1941.

I was disappointed in myself as well as the team. I thought we'd do better, and I thought I'd be a better manager than I was that first year.

In retrospect, I realize I was still learning. That first year I wasn't always alert enough to be thinking an inning or two ahead, which a good manager must do. It probably was because I was concentrating on playing my own position.

Something else I realize in looking back at my career, is that I couldn't understand why all of my players didn't play the game the same way I did. I don't mean with the same ability, but with the same determination, the same aggressiveness, the same will to win that I always had. There were times I was intolerant of my players for that reason, though I did my best to keep it within me, to not let it out publicly.

While the 1942 season was a disappointment for me as a manager, it was a good year personally. I hit .283 and made the All-Star team for the third straight time. I played all nine innings of the All-Star game in the Polo Grounds, hit a home run off Mort Cooper and handled nine chances in the field as we beat the National League, 3-1.

My second-base partner was Joe Gordon, then of the Yankees, and Cobbledick wrote the next day, "If Boudreau and Gordon could play together for a full season, they would overshadow every pair from Tinker and Evers down to the present. Their double play in the first inning was faster than the lightning that had been flashing around the Polo Grounds a few minutes earlier."

It was prophetic of Cobbledick, as five years later Gordon and I would play together, for four seasons, though his prediction might have been something of an exaggeration.

Because the American League beat the National League, we also played an all-star team of servicemen led by Bob Feller on July 7 at Cleveland Stadium.

We beat the servicemen, 5-0, in front of 62,094, and nearly $150,000 was raised for the Army-Navy relief fund. I went 0-for-

2, flying out against Feller, who gave up three runs in the first inning and was the losing pitcher.

The season was a learning year for me. It also was a challenge.

When I went home that October I asked myself, if I were the owner or general manager of the Indians, would I fire Lou Boudreau the manager?

Or would I want him back for the second season of his two-year contract?

I answered that I wouldn't fire Lou Boudreau, but I'd expect improvement in 1943.

Wartime Baseball

Wartime baseball was difficult for everybody—except those who couldn't have made it as major league players in normal times. It was especially difficult for the managers because we never knew who would be called into service next.

And because of the uncertainty, the draft boards had the greatest control over our destiny, greater than our managerial competence, or the ability of our players to pitch, hit, and field.

By the time the 1943 season started, more than 200 major leaguers were wearing Uncle Sam's uniform instead of baseball flannels, including many of the best players in the game—among them Joe DiMaggio, Ted Williams, and Hank Greenberg, as well as our Bob Feller.

It was still called "major league" baseball, but I'd have to say the caliber of the game in 1943, 1944, and 1945 was Triple-A, at best, maybe only Double-A.

The best example was Pete Gray, who played the outfield and batted .218 in 77 games for the St. Louis Browns in 1945, even though he had only one arm.

Actually, it's remarkable that Gray could do as well as he did, especially as a hitter, but also as the Browns' left fielder. It's certainly not my intention to denigrate Gray by citing him as an extreme example; he deserved a lot of credit. Considering his handicap, Gray played very well and was a favorite of the fans. From what I saw of him there's no doubt he would have been a great player, certainly a bona fide major leaguer, if he'd not lost an arm as a child.

Paul O'Dea was another. He was a promising young hitter and outfielder who'd had solid minor league credentials, but was blinded in the right eye in a spring training mishap in 1940. The accident forced Paul out of baseball that season, but he was a very courageous and determined guy. He refused to quit and made a comeback in the minors.

We brought O'Dea up in 1944 and he hit .318 in 76 games, which might have been even more amazing than what Pete Gray was able to do. But the pitchers soon caught up to Paul. His average fell off to .235 in 87 games in 1945 and, like Gray, he couldn't cut it when the regular players came back from the war.

Despite the lower caliber of baseball, we all were grateful the game was allowed to continue during those war years. The fact that every team had similar problems was a consolation and helped keep the competitive level fairly even, though the New York Yankees continued to dominate the American League, just as the St. Louis Cardinals did in the National League.

As for the Indians, we had struggled the final month of 1942 and wanted to make some changes, but were limited in what could be done. The only significant deal that Roger Peckinpaugh made was to trade center fielder Roy Weatherly and utility infielder Oscar Grimes to the Yankees for outfielder Roy Cullenbine and catcher Buddy Rosar.

Weatherly was a pretty good player but his average had steadily declined since 1939, when he batted .310. He also was a temperamental fellow and, while I had no problem with him, he had several run-ins with Peckinpaugh in 1941.

Because of the manpower shortage, Jim Bagby, one of our best pitchers, was to be a backup second baseman, and three other pitchers—Al Smith, Al Milnar, and Allie Reynolds—practiced in the outfield in case they were needed there; and yet another pitcher, Chubby Dean, was penciled in as one of my pinch-hitters.

Something else that happened during the winter of 1942-43 was that Commissioner Kenesaw Landis decreed that all teams conduct spring training north of the Mason-Dixon Line for the duration of the war.

It was done, he said, to curtail southern travel, though I could never figure out how we would have harmed the war effort by going back to Florida for spring training.

But that wasn't for me to worry about and everybody made the best of the situation—except Jeff Heath.

We took over the field house at Purdue University at West Lafayette, Indiana, for spring training. We chose Purdue over the University of Illinois because Peckinpaugh felt there would be too many distractions for me at my alma mater. I agreed, though it would have been nice to go "home."

Heath, like Weatherly, was another who had great potential, but whose temperament also detracted from his ability. He could have been a star, but never was. Heath held out until two days before the 1943 season started, and that hurt our hopes for getting off to a good start.

Because of Heath's holdout, he missed all the fun and games at Purdue (which might have been by design). He didn't agree to contract terms and rejoin us until we got to Cleveland for the opener against Detroit.

The Tigers came to town under a new manager, my old friend and former mentor, Steve O'Neill, who replaced Del Baker. And to complete the cycle, Baker, who had been fired by the Tigers, joined us as a coach to replace my old friend, Oscar Melillo.

It was Baker who was hailed as a genius when he piloted the Tigers to the pennant only three years earlier, which says plenty for the way a manager's fortunes change and the way the game often is played in the front offices.

I hated to see Melillo leave, because of our long-standing friendship, but Peckinpaugh wanted him to go into scouting, a job that Melillo handled very well. The addition of Baker meant I was still surrounded by experienced coaches as Burt Shotton and George Susce remained on the staff.

Jim Bagby, who had beaten the Tigers in my 1942 managerial debut and also in our last game of the season, did it again in the 1943 opener. Not only did he pitch well, a three-hitter, Bagby also got two hits himself and drove in the only run of the game with a ninth-inning sacrifice fly.

It was another great start for the Indians and their "Boy Manager," though news from the war sobered much of the elation we otherwise felt.

Sharing the headlines with our victory on the front page of the *Plain Dealer* the next morning, April 22, was a report that Japan had executed several American airmen who were downed and captured after they had conducted the first bombing raid on Tokyo several months earlier.

It brought us back to earth in a hurry. And while we wanted to play well and win, we were reminded—as we would be for three more years—that there were more important things happening in the world than major league pennant races.

We had one of the brightest young pitching prospects in the league in rookie Allie Reynolds. Also pitching well were Bagby and Al Smith, though Mel Harder, who at 34 was getting up in years, was not having a good season. We'd also lost Les Fleming, the first baseman who had played so well as a rookie in 1942. He put his baseball career on hold to work in a shipyard to get a deferment from the draft.

As it turned out, the American League race didn't last long for us. About two months, that's all.

We were fairly consistent through the first five weeks and even moved into first place for a few days in late May. It lulled me into the belief that we could make a run for the pennant, which turned out to be only a reflection of my inexperience.

As they say, a pennant race is a marathon, not a sprint, and we hit the skids, falling all the way to seventh place by mid-June. It was discouraging, though in retrospect I should have known we weren't good enough to be a contender. Not yet.

We rallied toward the end of the season and I thought we were coming together as a team. In mid-August we climbed out of fifth place into second, though we couldn't hold it and wound up third, 15 1/2 games behind the Yankees.

But our record was 82-71, eleven games over .500, and we finished only two games out of second place.

I felt that our strong showing under difficult circumstances, combined with my personal record, proved what I had been saying all along, that I could handle both jobs—managing the Indians and playing shortstop—and do both of them well.

In fact, I could have made a case for myself that I had become a better player since my appointment as manager.

I hit .286 in 1943, led all American League shortstops in fielding, and made the All-Star team for the fourth consecutive year (though I didn't get into the game, which the American League won, 5-3).

Alva Bradley and Roger Peckinpaugh must have agreed. Before I left Cleveland that fall they gave me a new two-year contract through 1945, with a raise to $25,000 for managing and $12,000 for playing each season.

While I was happy with my contract and what I considered to be a bright future for the team and myself, those 71 losses meant that I had been very unhappy at least 71 times during the previous season.

I confess to having been a very hard loser.

And if I were still involved as a player or manager, I'd still be the same. I never learned to be a good loser, though I handled it better once I had more experience. I would take a loss out on myself, in my office, usually alone. Sometimes I'd talk it out with one of my coaches and criticize myself. I'd get it over with, get it out of my system, then go home.

By the time the 1944 season was in full swing, I was able to leave the game at the park, not take it home with me if we lost—which was good because we lost a lot that year.

I felt pretty good at the start because the better teams in the league were coming back to us. New York, Boston, and Chicago were losing players to the service and I really thought we could make a move on them.

But it didn't happen.

Jim Bagby fell apart and won only four games (after winning 17 in each of the two previous seasons). Mel Harder made a comeback, winning 12 games (though that would be his last winning year). And Allie Reynolds went 11-8 but didn't develop as quickly as Peckinpaugh and I had anticipated.

We started out poorly and finished poorly—and in between we were even worse, falling into last place at the end of June with a 31-40 record.

It was discouraging for Lou Boudreau the manager, though Lou Boudreau the shortstop was having a great season.

By mid-season I was involved in a race for the batting championship with five other players: Snuffy Stirnweiss of the Yankees; Bobby Doerr, Bob Johnson, Pete Fox of the Red Sox, and Stan Spence of Washington.

Stirnweiss was leading the pack at .331 at the end of August, and I was fifth in the race with .315. Then everything clicked for me. From September 1 through the end of the season, October 2, I hit .371.

It boosted me into second with a .316 mark on September 7; I gained a point to .317 and was still second on September 14, and a week later I was up to .321, but still second, seven percentage points behind Johnson.

Suddenly my "race" became bigger news than the pennant race, which was good because unfortunately, we had been out of contention since June. We were a weak fifth, trying desperately to stay ahead of Philadelphia and Chicago, so it was just as well that the attention was focused on me, not the team.

St. Louis, under the leadership of our former coach, Luke Sewell, had the Browns in first place in a close race with Detroit, managed by Steve O'Neill.

Both races went down to the final day.

The Browns won the pennant by beating the Yankees, 5-3. The star of that St. Louis team was a shortstop named Vernon "Junior" Stephens, whom we'll hear more about later.

I won the batting championship with a hit in my final trip to the plate for a .327 mark, two points higher than Doerr and three more than Johnson. Stirnweiss finished at .319 and Spence at .316.

It was personally gratifying to do that well. I also set a new fielding record for shortstops with a .978 percentage and participated in 134 double plays, most ever by a shortstop until then.

But my team finishing in a fifth-place tie with Philadelphia was disappointing, especially after we'd done so well the year before. We thought we'd turned the corner and were on our way to the top.

For the first time I had some doubts about myself, though I wouldn't admit it to anybody, not even Della.

Maybe it was because we'd done so well in 1943 and I thought I knew it all.

Or maybe I had concentrated too much on being a good player, on winning the batting championship, and didn't bear down enough to be a good manager.

I wasn't sure, though Mr. Bradley and Peckinpaugh were very tolerant—but wouldn't be if it happened again in 1945.

I turned it into another challenge.

In those days the Indians were practically a traveling team all season, which didn't make it easy. The mammoth downtown Municipal Stadium was opened in July 1932. We played all our home games there in 1933, but in 1934 and continuing for 13 seasons, we went back and forth between the Stadium, with a capacity of nearly 80,000, and cozy little League Park, built in 1891, that seated only about 21,000.

We never felt like we were at home because both parks were so different.

Forty-two of our 77 home games were played at Municipal Stadium in 1945. Sometimes, depending on the attraction, a game would be switched from League Park to the stadium, or vice versa, even the day before it was to be played. It was very hectic for the players, the clubhouse attendant, and the traveling secretary—not to mention the manager. I'm sure it was confusing for the fans, too.

Pitchers loved the stadium, but the hitters—especially Jeff Heath—hated it, all with good reason. Prior to 1947 there were no interior fences. The playing field was expansive: 320 feet down the foul lines and curving drastically to 420 feet in center field.

On the other hand, League Park was a field of dreams for left-handed batters, though a field of nightmares for right-handers. The distance to the right-field foul pole was only 290 feet, but it was 375 to left and 420 to center.

That close right-field fence at League Park was part of the reason I developed what a lot of people considered a strange batting stance. I held my bat high, but crouched at the knees and waist to help me hit to right field on the advice of Johnny Bassler, one of our coaches when I came up to the Indians from Buffalo in 1939.

As determined as I was to make 1945 a good season for both the Indians and me, we started badly again and got worse before getting better—with good reason.

Ken Keltner entered the Navy and we started the year with an outfielder, Roy Cullenbine, playing third base. My second base buddy, Ray Mack, went into the Army. Heath, who wanted to be traded (and got his wish the following winter), and catcher Buddy Rosar were holdouts the first six weeks of the season. And Mel Harder also joined us late. He'd been working in a war plant and didn't pitch his first game until July 1.

The draft board came after me, too. I was reclassified on May 3 and ordered to report for a physical on June 15, which I failed again because of my ankles.

The opener, which we lost to Chicago, 5-2, was an embarrassment to me, even though I went 4-for-4 against Lefty Lee. The White Sox third baseman, Tony Cuccinello (who would lead the league in hitting most of the season), pulled the old hidden ball trick on me in the sixth inning. I was tagged out at third base and

I was humiliated because it killed a rally—and certainly didn't help my control over the players, to whom I'd always preached the importance of being alert at all times.

In retrospect, I probably should have fined myself.

We lost six of our first seven games, and by late June, when we were stuck in seventh place with a 21-29 record, I handed out some stiff fines to three or four players for their failure to hustle. I hated to do it, but something was needed.

Maybe it did some good as we started to play a little better and climbed up to .500 for the first time on July 31, when our record evened at 44-44, though we were still down in fifth place.

Fleming rejoined us on August 1, and we got over .500 at 49-48 for the first time on August 8.

We climbed into fourth place on August 13, the day before the Japanese surrendered in World War II, which also was the day disaster struck and ended my season as a player.

I was covering second base when big Dolph Camilli of the Red Sox slid hard to break up a double play. It happened in the second inning of a game we won, 3-0. My brittle right ankle snapped. It was broken and I was finished for the season with a .306 average.

What a lousy way to celebrate the end of the war—and the return of Bob Feller from the war!

Feller was discharged a week later, after 44 months in the Navy. He'd spent 27 months as a gunnery specialist aboard the battleship U.S.S. *Alabama,* and came home wearing eight battle stars.

It was appropriate that Feller's opponent in his first start, August 24, was Hal Newhouser, who was considered—in Feller's absence, of course—the greatest pitcher in the game at the time. Newhouser had won 29 games for Detroit in 1944, and would go 25-9 in 1945.

It also was appropriate that Bob struck out the first batter he faced that night, Jimmy Outlaw, on a 3-and-2 pitch that set off a cascade of cheers that rocked the stadium. The "Strikeout King" was back!

Urged on by the 46,477 partisan fans who turned out to welcome him back from the war, Feller limited Detroit to four hits and struck out 12 to beat Newhouser and the Tigers, 4-2.

We made a final sprint, thanks to the presence of Feller, and by August 27 we were only six and a half games out of first place, though there were four teams ahead of us—the Tigers, Washington, St. Louis, and New York.

Feller won four more of his nine starts for a 5-3 record before the curtain fell on my fourth season as manager of the Indians. This one was doubly disappointing.

Though we finished 73-72, one game over .500, an improvement over 1944, we failed to contend for the pennant. My streak of leading the American League shortstops in fielding also was stopped for the first time in six seasons.

I made only nine errors in over 500 chances and my fielding percentage was .983, the highest of my major league career. But it didn't qualify because I'd played only 97 games, three fewer than the required minimum, thanks to that broken ankle.

Little wonder I was looking forward to better things in 1946, especially with the war being over and the return of *real* major league baseball—as well as the return from the war of a man whose presence would have a great impact on my career, and on baseball in Cleveland.

Hello, Bill

I wasn't happy with my record as a manager—fourth in 1942, third in 1943, tied for fifth in 1944 and fifth in 1945—but I hoped that Alva Bradley and Roger Peckinpaugh understood how difficult it was to manage during the war.

Players came and went at the will of their draft boards, and I felt I'd done the best job possible under the circumstances.

Fortunately, Mr. Bradley and Peck agreed and gave me another two-year contract. They even granted me a raise to $45,000 a year, which included $25,000 for managing and $20,000 for playing shortstop. It was gratifying to know they were satisfied that I was handling both jobs okay.

But I knew going into the 1946 season that it was time to start producing, and I made sure my players were aware of it, too. I really believed we were good enough to win the pennant that season, and told them I wouldn't ask anybody to do anything I wasn't willing to do myself.

Because the wartime travel restrictions were lifted, major league teams were allowed to return to Florida for spring training. That was another great relief, too.

We opened camp in Clearwater and welcomed what seemed to be a cast of thousands, though some familiar faces were among the missing, mainly outfielder Jeff Heath and pitcher Jim Bagby.

It's true, as was speculated at the time, that neither Bagby, Heath, nor Hayes were favorites of mine. Heath was a loner, very unpredictable, not an easy guy for anybody to get along with. I never cared much for Bagby, the way he acted, and Hayes was getting up in years.

But the main reason Peck traded all of them was simply that we felt we had better young players coming in.

Most of the fellows who'd gone off to the service were returning to reclaim their jobs, and we also had a good crop of rookies getting their first chance to play in the big leagues.

Our nucleus was pretty good, headed by Bob Feller. While the rest of our starting pitching staff was young, we thought it would be good with Steve Gromek, Allie Reynolds, and Red Embree. Mel Harder was still with us, though he would not be a factor and would retire in another year.

Ray Mack, Ken Keltner, Les Fleming, and Hank Edwards were back, and among the good-looking guys fresh out of the service were catcher Jim Hegan, outfielder Gene Woodling, and a third baseman named Bob Lemon.

Yes, *that* Bob Lemon. I'll tell you more about him later.

My coaching staff also was different. Burt Shotton had asked to be reassigned to scouting, which he did out of his home in Lake Wales, Florida. A year later Shotton would return to managing, which he wanted to do from the time he applied for the job I got in 1941, and lead the Brooklyn Dodgers to the 1947 and 1949 National League pennants.

We didn't replace Shotton immediately, though Buster Mills, who'd played briefly for us in 1942 before he went into the service, became a player/coach by the time the season started. Mills was then 37 years old and couldn't compete much as a player with the younger guys on the roster.

Old friend Oscar Melillo was back, having replaced Del Baker, who resigned in 1945; and George Susce, who was with me from the beginning of my managerial career, was still on the staff.

We made a lot of changes that spring and had close to 60 different players in uniform at one time or another. Looking back at it I should have known it was going to be *that* kind of a year.

Nobody was picking us to win the pennant, but everybody with the club—perhaps most of all, Bradley and Peckinpaugh—expected an interesting season.

How right they were, though not necessarily for the reasons they had in mind.

One problem that surfaced immediately was the realization that we desperately needed a center fielder, which is how Bob Lemon first came into prominence.

Because we were desperate, and also because Ken Keltner was firmly entrenched at third base, I decided to give Lemon, the rookie third baseman, a chance to play the outfield. He'd hit well in the minors, had a strong arm, could run, and was a good judge of fly balls.

Lemon had done some pitching in the Navy, but wanted to play every day and was more than willing to switch positions in order to get into the starting lineup.

It was a move that paid off immediately—though not for the long run—as we beat Chicago, 1-0, in the opener. Lemon made a sensational game-saving catch to preserve the victory for Feller.

On the basis of that first game, it seemed that our center field problem was solved for a long time.

Unfortunately it wasn't, as Lemon failed to hit consistently—but that proved to be a blessing in disguise.

As everyone knows, Lemon became one of the best pitchers in the game, though the conversion didn't happen immediately, and not without considerable resistance on his part.

But Lemon wasn't the only one who didn't hit, and our offense was very inoffensive, to say the least. We lost five of our first nine games and, by the first week of May, we'd fallen into seventh place.

Even Bob Feller was struggling. He won only one of his first three starts and there was talk around the league that the famous "Strikeout King" had left his fastball in the Navy.

But Feller, great competitor that he was, proved the doomsayers wrong without a shadow of a doubt. We went into New York, where the critics were chirping the loudest, and Feller shut them up by pitching his second career no-hitter, on April 30.

But it didn't come easily, and not without great suspense.

Feller beat the Yankees, 1-0, our only run coming on a ninth-inning homer by Frankie Hayes off Floyd Bevens. It would be Hayes's last significant contribution as he was traded to the Chicago White Sox by the time we got into June.

Nobody was thinking no-hitter in the first inning when I was fortunate enough to make a play on a hot grounder that Snuffy Stirnweiss hit to the right side of second base. I somehow reached the ball and, while in the process of falling, made an underhand throw to Les Fleming at first base. My momentum forced me into a somersault and I landed on my back—but Stirnweiss was out.

The Yankees threatened to break the no-hitter in the eighth and ninth, and I've always been proud that Ray Mack and I were able to make a couple of key plays to preserve it for Feller.

With two out in the eighth, Phil Rizzuto slashed a grounder that normally would have gone through the hole between short and third, into left field. Because nobody was on base, I was playing Rizzuto to pull and was shaded toward third.

I'm the first to admit that I was not the fastest shortstop, and I certainly didn't have the best legs and ankles. But I studied opposing hitters and positioned myself, depending on my pitcher and what he was throwing.

It turned out that I played Rizzuto just right, though I still had to go deep into the hole to field his grounder and then make a fast, hard throw to get him at first base by half a step.

Then in the bottom of the ninth, after Hayes's homer, the Yankees threatened to not only break the no-hitter, but win the game.

Stirnweiss led off with a bunt that Les Fleming fumbled for an error, and Tommy Henrich sacrificed. That brought Joe DiMaggio to the plate with the tying run in scoring position. I hoped DiMaggio would hit the ball to me, which he did. But not until Feller had gone to a 3-and-2 count, keeping the fans on the edge of their seats, and all of us on our toes.

I fielded DiMaggio's grounder and threw him out. It moved Stirnweiss to third and brought up Charlie "King Kong" Keller, a hard-hitting, left-handed batter.

Now it was Mack's turn to come through for Feller, which he did—but again, not without one last thrill.

In his anxiety to field Keller's grounder, Mack stumbled and fell to his knees. If he had not recovered in time and Keller had reached, I'm positive it would have been ruled an error. But it also would have enabled Stirnweiss to score from third, tying the game and, of course, prolonging it.

But Mack wouldn't give up on the ball and while still on his knees, threw out Keller to end the game.

Feller would go on to pitch three no-hitters, as well as 12 one-hitters, in his great career, and I am absolutely convinced he would have won 30 games in 1946 if we had given him better support. As it was, Bob's record that season was 26-15, and he pitched the remarkable total of 371 innings.

The magnitude of that achievement takes on greater significance when it is considered that only two pitchers since 1946 have worked that many innings in a single season—Wilbur Wood, a knuckleballer for the White Sox, who pitched 377 innings in 1972, and Mickey Lolich of Detroit, 376 in 1971.

There was not much to cheer about the next several weeks as we fell into last place, which was very discouraging because my hopes had been so high. We managed to climb into fifth by mid-June, and won four straight to raise our record to 26-32 on June 21, when one of the biggest events in Cleveland baseball history took place.

Bill Veeck bought the Indians.

He'd arrived in town around the middle of June, initially identified himself only as "Mr. Edwards," then as "Mr. Lewis," and asked a lot of general questions about sports in Cleveland, and the Indians in particular.

But there had not been any speculation that the Indians might be up for sale until it was splashed across the top of the *Plain Dealer* on June 19. The story reported that Veeck was trying to negotiate a deal with Alva Bradley, who was the major stockholder in the group that had owned the club since November 17, 1927.

The news hit like a bombshell, and nobody was more interested than I, for obvious reasons.

It was reported that Veeck and his primary partner, Harry Grabiner, a former Chicago White Sox executive, probably would want Jimmy Dykes as manager if they were successful in buying the Indians. Three and a half weeks earlier Dykes had resigned as manager of the White Sox, a job he'd held since 1934.

Veeck subsequently denied his intention to bring Dykes to Cleveland, but his remarks, as reported in the *Plain Dealer* were hardly a vote of confidence for me.

"It's my opinion that the Indians should be higher in the race than they are," he was quoted as saying. "There are weaknesses, however, and if I am successful in my attempt to gain control of the club, my first official step will be to correct those weaknesses."

When the reporter asked about my status, it was stated, "Veeck lauded Manager Lou Boudreau as a 'swell fellow and a great player.'" But he said nothing good or bad about my managerial ability.

Later in the story, when asked specifically about Dykes, Veeck said he felt "very friendly toward Jimmy," but maintained that he had not discussed the possibility of Dykes taking over as manager of the Indians.

During Veeck's negotiations with Bradley, I kept a low profile and concentrated on running the team, though it was difficult.

Through it all, I never even met Veeck until after the deal was finalized on June 21. It was then that Veeck and Grabiner immediately "accepted" Roger Peckinpaugh's resignation as general manager. Peck said he didn't mind, that he didn't blame Veeck, knowing that the new owner planned to be his own general manager.

As for me, I knew that Veeck, Grabiner, and another prominent stockholder, Bob Goldstein, felt that the club would improve with another manager, and my playing would also improve if I were relieved of the extra burden of running the team.

Shortly after Veeck closed the deal, we had a dinner meeting in his hotel room. "You probably want to know exactly where you stand, and I'm going to be very frank with you," he started the discussion about my future.

"We know about your ball playing. You're the best, and that's putting it mildly. But we have some doubts about your managerial ability. We have no plans to change managers immediately. We may never change. We're going to wait and see. Meanwhile, you're the manager and don't worry about anything else."

But of course I did and I made it clear that if I were relieved as manager, I would have to be traded, that I would not play for the Indians under another manager.

My new employers accepted my ultimatum at face value and everybody seemed to be satisfied to let it go at that—though there was no doubt in my mind that I was on trial as a manager, and would be for the rest of the season at least.

Veeck was like a whirlwind once he got situated in Cleveland. We always had three teams—one on the field, another coming, and one going. We never had the same team on the field for more than a week at a time.

But players weren't all that Veeck brought in. There were vaudeville acts and fireworks displays, and one giveaway after another. He also hired a couple of baseball clowns, Jackie Price and Max Patkin. They were comical and talented in their own right, but were an almost constant distraction.

They also distracted the fans' attention away from our losing games, which probably was Veeck's motive.

Price had some ability as an infielder and Veeck wanted me to get him into the lineup. I resisted as best I could, though we did use him in seven games. He batted thirteen times and even got three infield hits. Patkin was hilarious coaching at first base, which I let him do on occasion—when he couldn't do any damage.

The pot was kept boiling by Veeck, who felt that as long as we weren't in contention for the pennant, he had to find other ways to generate excitement, entertain the fans. And they were entertained. Call it a "diversionary tactic," as one reporter wrote.

When Veeck took over the franchise on June 21, we were 17 games behind Boston, in fifth place with a 26-33 record, a .441 winning percentage.

When the season ended, we finished 36 games behind the Red Sox, at 68-86, a winning percentage of .442.

I didn't know if Veeck blamed me, though it would be an issue I'd have to face soon enough.

At the time, and through the rest of that season, our relationship was friendly, at least on the surface. He kept telling me not to worry about what I'd be reading in the papers, and I didn't.

I concentrated on proving to Veeck the things I felt I'd already proved—that I could handle both jobs well.

While we were never able to climb above fifth place, I had another good season, hitting .293 and leading American League shortstops in fielding again.

Despite my good statistics, I didn't make the All-Star team.

But it was my own fault this time, which resulted in what I considered an even greater honor bestowed upon me by Veeck.

In those days the managers in the league chose the All-Star players, but I didn't vote for myself as the American League shortstop. I named Vernon Stephens, who would hit .307 with 14 homers and 64 runs batted in for the St. Louis Browns.

I guess I expected that my old friend Steve O'Neill, who would manage the American Leaguers, would pick me as an alternate. I was surprised when he didn't.

So was Veeck. Surprised and angered to the extent that he complained to American League President William Harridge.

According to a column in the *Plain Dealer*, Gordon Cobbledick said he observed Veeck telling Harridge, "Everybody knows Boudreau is the best shortstop in baseball. It isn't fair to him or to the Cleveland fans or to me and my stockholders to leave him off the All-Star squad.

"It also isn't fair to the league because we'd certainly have a better team with him in there than without him. Isn't there something you can do about it?" Veeck asked Harridge.

Apparently there wasn't—so Veeck did the next best thing. He gave me a "night," which was a popular way to recognize favorite players in those days.

He also presented me with a huge trophy that was inscribed, "To The Greatest Shortstop Ever Left Off The All-Star Team."

Whether it was Veeck's way of exploiting the situation to draw a crowd at my expense, or a sincere gesture on his part, it was appreciated.

It was about the same time, the middle of the season, that I did something that pleased Veeck, though my motives were selfish.

Ted Williams, back after three years in the service, was beating our brains out every time we played the Red Sox. Of course, he was beating the brains out of everybody and would go on to hit .342, win the American League's Most Valuable Player award and lead the Red Sox to the pennant.

It was in early July, after Williams had killed us again in a game at League Park with its short right-field fence, that I dreamed up a plan to stop him, or at least nullify some of his power. Charts that we kept on opposing batters showed that 95 percent of Williams's hits were to right field.

My plan was predicated on the belief that Williams, who made no secret of the fact that he wanted to be known as the greatest hitter of all time—which I think he was—would be too proud to adjust his style to counteract my strategy, that it would be beneath his dignity to change.

I called it the "Boudreau Shift," though others refer to it as the "Williams Shift."

When I told my coaches what I had in mind, they scoffed. "You can't do that, it's crazy, it's never been done before," they told me.

I said I believed it would work because, knowing Williams's disposition, he would take it as a personal challenge.

And I vowed, "When the time is right, we'll do it."

That time came about 10 days later, and I was right. Williams considered it a personal affront, a challenge to his ability as a great hitter.

My plan was to overload the right side of the infield and outfield, leaving the left side open. I wanted Williams to try to beat the shift by hitting into it, where we had six players stationed, or to swallow his pride and go to the opposite field where his hits would be less meaningful. Even if he bunted along the third-base side, it would be fine with me.

We went into Boston on July 14 for a doubleheader at Fenway Park. I had a great game in the opener—5-for-5 with four doubles and a home run for 12 total bases. My five extra-base hits were a major league record.

But Williams went 4-for-5 with three homers, all to right field, and drove in eight runs. We lost, 11-10.

My French blood was all stirred up. So was my French vocabulary. I was angry, upset, and determined to stop Williams.

I held a meeting between games and told my players, "Anytime Williams comes up with the bases empty and you hear me yell 'Yo!' this is what I want you to do," and I diagrammed the shift on a chalkboard.

I stationed our first baseman, Jimmy Wasdell that day, and the right fielder, Hank Edwards, virtually on the right-field foul line. I moved the second baseman, Jack Conway, much closer to first and back on the grass, placed myself to the right of second base, and had third baseman Ken Keltner play directly behind second on the edge of the outfield grass. Pat Seerey, our center fielder that day, moved far to the right, covering the area normally patrolled by the right fielder.

It left us with only the left fielder, George Case, on that side of the field, and he was stationed about 30 feet closer than normal, practically playing a deep shortstop.

The reaction of my players was predictable. Most of them laughed because they thought I was kidding. I assured them I wasn't.

One of them said, "Hell, Lou, he'll just bunt."

I said, "Fine. I hope he does." And I did.

We sprang it on Williams the second time he batted in the second game. It was the third inning and he came up with nobody on base. I cupped my hands and yelled, "Yo!" All my guys looked at me, but waited until I made the first move. Then they followed.

Williams stepped out of the batter's box, turned around to umpire Bill Summers and said, "What the hell is going on out there . . . they can't do that," my catcher Sherman Lollar told me later.

Summers looked, chuckled, and told Williams, "As long as they have nine guys on the field and eight of them are inside the foul lines, they can play anywhere they please."

Lollar said Williams cursed, then joined in the laughter and got back in the batter's box. Williams squeezed the bat so hard Lollar said he looked for sawdust to come out of the handle. Red Embree, our pitcher, went to a 1-and-1 count and Williams grounded to me where the second baseman would normally be playing.

We used the shift once more that game, in the sixth inning, the only time Williams came up again with the bases empty. This time Embree walked him.

Afterwards Williams was quoted as saying, "If everybody starts playing me like that, I guess I'll have to turn around and hit right handed," which would have been fine with me.

We lost the game, 6-4, but I was satisfied the shift would work to our advantage more often than not. I planned to use it again, which I often did, even though it backfired on us later that season.

We went into the shift in the very first inning of a game on September 13 at League Park. Embree again was our pitcher and Williams deliberately poked a pitch into left field.

It was only a routine fly, but with Seerey, our left fielder that day, playing what amounted to a deep shortstop, the ball soared over his head. Williams rounded the bases for his first ever—and I believe *only*—inside-the-park homer.

Embree allowed only one other hit the rest of the game, but we couldn't score against Tex Hughson and the Red Sox won, 1-0.

And to add insult to injury, at least in Williams's mind, it was that victory that clinched the pennant for the Red Sox.

But I didn't care, and as long as Williams was stubborn enough to challenge it, which he did most of the time, the shift helped us. Our charts showed that we were 37 percent more successful when we used the shift against Williams than when we didn't.

I always considered the "Boudreau Shift" against Williams a psychological, if not always a tactical, victory.

Williams never said anything to me about it, not even when I went over to manage the Red Sox in 1952. But the clubhouse attendant in Boston, Johnny Orlando, told me that Ted would really get teed off, which again was part of my strategy.

As much as Williams hated the shift, Veeck loved it. Maybe even more. It was the kind of thing he would have done if he'd thought of it first, to divert attention from a mediocre ball club.

After Bob Feller's no-hitter on April 30, he was off and running toward the major league season strikeout record which was then considered to be 343 set by Rube Waddell in 1904. By the time August rolled around, we—and especially Veeck—knew that Feller had the record in sight.

Feller reached a career high of 262 strikeouts in 261 2/3 innings on August 13, in a night game at the stadium against Detroit. It had taken him 320 1/3 innings to record his previous best in 1940.

Veeck loved it and we decided that Bob would pitch as often as he felt capable of it. We were out of pennant contention and didn't really have any place to go in the standings, though we continued to try to win as many games as possible to stay out of seventh place.

Feller's quest went down to the wire. While pitching in relief in our second-to-last game, Bob tied what was listed as Waddell's record with four strikeouts in a 9-8 victory over Detroit on September 27.

Everybody, including Feller—and *especially* Veeck—wanted to see Feller break the record so I started him in our last game though he'd be working with only two days' rest.

The Tigers' starter was Hal Newhouser, Feller's chief rival as the best pitcher in baseball, and it was appropriate that these two aces would wind up at the end of the season with so much on the line. Not only was Feller going for the strikeout record, he also was trying to win his twenty-sixth game. Newhouser was seeking his twenty-seventh victory.

It was even more appropriate that Feller's first strikeout victim that day, the strikeout that broke Waddell's 42-year-old record, was none other than Newhouser. Feller went on to strike out four more batters, the last one being Jimmy Bloodworth in the ninth inning for a record 348, and a 4-1 victory.

It was a great personal triumph for Feller, as he also led the American League that season in five other departments: shutouts, innings pitched, games started, games pitched, and complete games.

So much for those doomsayers who thought he was washed up!

Feller's season inspired researchers to recheck Waddell's game-by-game performances in 1904. They discovered that he had not been credited with six strikeouts, which raised his record to 349, one more than Feller got in 1946. However, at the time and for several years later, Bob was considered the record holder.

Since then Sandy Koufax and Nolan Ryan both have broken the single-season strikeout record, Koufax with 382 in 1965, and Ryan with 383 in 1973, but I don't believe there ever was a better, more dominating pitcher in baseball than Bob Feller in his prime.

Everybody talked about Feller's fastball, and rightfully so. It was once clocked at 108 miles per hour. But he also developed a great curveball which, in the latter stages of his career, became his best pitch.

One pitcher who came close to being as dominating as Feller was Bob Lemon—yes, that same Bob Lemon who came up with us as a third baseman and started the 1946 season as our center fielder. The same Bob Lemon whose sensational, diving catch saved Feller's 1-0 victory over Chicago on Opening Day.

I knew Lemon had a strong arm, and once I realized he was not going to hit with consistency as an outfielder, I thought it would be worthwhile to look at him as a pitcher.

Lemon had done some pitching in the Navy. I asked Bill Dickey, the Yankee catcher, who'd been in the service with Lemon, for his opinion. Dickey told me what I already knew, that it would be worth a try to see what he could do as a pitcher.

We eased Lemon in slowly the latter half of the season, when it was obvious we weren't going to be fighting for the pennant.

By then it also was evident that some of the pitchers we'd counted upon were not going to come through. Steve Gromek's record fell from 19-9 in 1945 to 5-15, Allie Reynolds went from 18-12 to 11-15, Red Embree didn't develop as expected and won only eight games while losing twelve, and Mel Harder, then 36 years old, was still having arm trouble and would pitch only 13 games, winning five and losing four.

I asked myself, why not give Lemon a look? What did we have to lose anyway? Veeck agreed, and Lemon made 32 appearances, 27 in relief. While he won only four games while losing five, his earned run average was a sparkling 2.49, offering more than enough hope that he could be a winning pitcher for us. How right we were.

I was glad when the season finally ended. It had been a long and eventful, sometimes tumultuous year with the arrival of Veeck and his promotional wizardry that kept the turnstiles clicking.

Attendance in 1946 was 1,057,289, largest in the history of the franchise—but only a beginning.

I was not satisfied with our performance and record on the field, but I was satisfied that we were making progress, that we'd turned the corner. I was sure the future looked bright for the Cleveland Indians.

But did it for me? I felt that Veeck and I made a pretty good pair, and that I had convinced him that I was a good manager as well as the "greatest shortstop ever left off the All-Star team."

How wrong I would prove to be.

We're Loyal To
You, Lou

Bill Veeck kept the pot boiling during the winter of 1946-47, but now the ingredients were different.

Sensing, as I did, that we were on the verge of becoming a good team, a contender, Bill concentrated more on adding good players than dreaming up stunts and gimmicks to attract the fans, though he continued to be a promotional genius.

It was during the 1946 World Series between Boston and the St. Louis Cardinals that Veeck addressed what he considered our greatest need, a run-producing second baseman. Ray Mack, who'd been a promising hitter when we started out together in Buffalo in 1939, never lived up to expectations.

In fact, after Mack rejoined us in 1946 from military duty, he batted a career-low .205 in 61 games. Much as I hated to do it because of our friendship, I replaced Ray at second base with Dutch Meyer, an infielder we obtained from Detroit. Meyer was a journeyman at best, but I felt he could do more for us than Mack.

When the season ended I agreed with Veeck that we needed somebody better than Meyer or Mack at second base if we were ever going to fight for a pennant.

Veeck, as shrewd a judge of talent as he was a promoter, fixed his eyes on Joe Gordon, a target I heartily endorsed. Gordon had won the American League's Most Valuable Player award in 1942, when he hit .322 with 18 homers and drove in 103 runs. But his average fell to .249 in 1943, before he went into the service for two years.

When Gordon returned to the New York Yankees in 1946 at the age of 31 and hit only .210 with 11 homers and 47 runs batted in, they assumed he was past his peak, washed up.

Besides, Gordon and Yankees president Larry MacPhail had a couple of run-ins during the season, and it was no secret that Manager Bucky Harris was planning to move Snuffy Stirnweiss from third to second base. It was as a second baseman in 1945, when Gordon was in the service, that Stirnweiss won the American League batting championship.

What's more, it also was common knowledge that the Yankees felt they needed another starting pitcher to regain the pennant, which they had not won since 1943. So the pieces for a trade started to fit perfectly together.

But not immediately. Veeck, playing his cards like a master wheeler-dealer—which he was—initially asked MacPhail for Stirnweiss, a .251 hitter in 1946. He offered hard-throwing right-hander Red Embree, who'd gone 8-12 for us, in exchange.

MacPhail was interested in Embree, but balked at giving up Stirnweiss, which Veeck expected. MacPhail countered with Gordon, which was exactly what Veeck hoped he'd do.

But before the deal could be consummated, MacPhail said he wanted to check with his people to make sure they agreed. Most of them did. But one who didn't was Joe DiMaggio.

DiMaggio told MacPhail that Allie Reynolds would be a better pitcher than Embree. He recommended that MacPhail not make the deal for Gordon unless Veeck would do it for Reynolds, who'd gone 11-15 in 1946.

Veeck reluctantly agreed because we were desperately in need of all the things Gordon could provide: power and clutch hitting, experience and on-field leadership. We also got utility infielder Eddie Bockman.

The deal was made on October 19 and turned out to be good for both of us.

Sure, Reynolds became the Yankees' best pitcher, winning 19 games and losing only eight in 1947, and leading them back to the World Series.

But Gordon also gave us exactly what we needed. He complemented me as I did him, and we became an even better shortstop-second base combination than Ray Mack and I had been.

Joe was happy to come to Cleveland because he'd been under such great pressure with the Yankees. He said everything was usually blown out of proportion in New York and he looked forward to playing for the Indians. It was nice to hear because not everybody felt that way about coming to Cleveland.

While the significance of the deal for Gordon cannot be minimized, Veeck and MacPhail pulled off another one exactly two months and a day later. It also turned out to be of major importance for us, though the newspapers called it a "minor transaction" then.

And again it was Veeck who played his cards exactly right, though this time he might have been more lucky than smart.

Veeck told MacPhail that, since trading Reynolds, we needed a young pitcher or two, and suggested the Yankees probably could use a backup catcher for then-untested Yogi Berra.

MacPhail listened as Veeck asked for a couple of young fellows our scouts had recommended, Al Gettel and Frank Shea.

Shea was then in the minors, though Gettel had been up with the Yankees in 1945 and 1946, but was not considered a frontliner.

Veeck offered Sherman Lollar, a rookie catcher who didn't figure in our plans. It was our intention to go with another youngster, named Jim Hegan, as our regular catcher, backed up by 38-year-old Al Lopez. We'd acquired Lopez a few weeks earlier in a deal with Pittsburgh for Gene Woodling. (Little did I realize then the significant role Lopez would play in my future.)

Veeck also offered Ray Mack, who had become expendable with our acquisition of Gordon.

MacPhail liked the idea of getting Lollar and figured Mack would be useful in a utility role. He was willing to give us Gettel, but not Shea. He put together a list of fifteen other minor league pitchers and told Veeck to pick one to go with Gettel.

A couple guys MacPhail was offering had pitched for the Oakland Oaks, a Yankee farm club in the Pacific Coast League managed by Casey Stengel. Veeck knew Stengel well; he had managed Veeck's Milwaukee Brewers a few years earlier.

So Veeck called Stengel and asked his advice. Stengel recommended a left-handed knuckleball pitcher named Gene Bearden. "Grab him before MacPhail regains his sanity," Stengel told Veeck.

But Bill wasn't finished. He went back to MacPhail and said Bearden would be acceptable, along with Gettel, but only if the Yankees threw in another player. He asked for a journeyman outfielder named Hal Peck, whose main claim to fame was that he could play ball despite having lost two toes on his right foot in a childhood accident.

I couldn't figure out why Veeck was determined to get Peck. He didn't have much of an arm, couldn't run very well and, I figured, would be only an extra outfielder at best. But Veeck told me he'd had Peck at Milwaukee and considered him a good-luck charm, and since we needed all the good fortune we could get, who was I to disagree?

So the deal went through on December 20—Bearden, Gettel, and Peck for Lollar and Mack.

But the acquisition of Gordon, Bearden, Gettel, and Peck was only the beginning.

The changes were coming fast and furious.

Even before the 1947 season began, Veeck decided we would no longer play at League Park because of its limited seating capacity. He had much bigger plans in mind.

In a way it was sad to abandon the old place, which had been "home" to Cleveland baseball teams since 1891, but I was glad because we all were tired of being a "traveling" team, going between League Park and Municipal Stadium for our games. The final game at League Park was played on September 21, 1946. We lost to Detroit, 5-3, in 11 innings in front of fewer than 3,000 spectators.

The stadium was a good place to play, especially after Veeck installed an outfield fence two weeks into the 1947 season. The fence initially was portable, that is, it could be moved in or out, which Veeck did depending upon the opposition. If a long-ball hitting team came in, he ordered the fences moved out. And for weaker-hitting teams, they were moved in. Anything to get even the slightest advantage.

It wasn't long, however, before American League president William Harridge instituted a rule stating the fence could not be moved, or removed, once the season started.

Something else Veeck changed in 1947 was our spring training headquarters. After travel restrictions were lifted at the end of World War II, we trained in Clearwater, Florida, which was okay, certainly an improvement over Purdue University at West Lafayette, Indiana.

Veeck, who owned a ranch outside Tucson, Arizona, made a deal with that city to build us a training complex. He also got Horace Stoneham, who owned the New York Giants, to move his team to Phoenix, Arizona, for spring training, and thus was born the "Cactus League."

We were the only teams in Arizona that first year, though the two Chicago teams trained in California, the White Sox in Pasadena and the Cubs on Catalina Island. Eventually several other teams moved to Arizona for spring training and the Indians remained in Tucson for 46 years.

We didn't bring Buster Mills back as a coach, but because Veeck felt the same as Bradley and Peckinpaugh about surrounding me with veteran baseball men, we hired Bill McKechnie, then 60, to join my staff with Oscar Melillo and George Susce. I didn't know McKechnie at the time—he had managed in the National League for 24 years, until he was fired by Cincinnati in 1946—but it was an excellent decision.

"Pops," as I called McKechnie, became like a father to me. He knew baseball as well as anybody I ever met, and had great influence on me and my career from that point on. I also give McKechnie credit for completing the transformation of Bob Lemon into one of the Indians'—and baseball's—best pitchers.

I knew that Pops had made a great pitcher out of Bucky Walters, who had come up through the Cincinnati Reds farm system as a third baseman, just as Lemon did in Cleveland.

I had seen enough of Lemon in 1946 to know that his future was neither as an infielder nor outfielder, but as a pitcher, and I turned him over to McKechnie.

"Pops," I told him in spring training, "I want you to take Lemon to the bullpen, look at him, work with him, and when he's ready to be a starting pitcher, let me know."

Not long after that, McKechnie came to me and said, "Louie," which is what he always called me, "You've got yourself a pretty good pitcher. . . . Lemon is ready."

He was right. Lemon went 11-5 that first season, and was a 20-game winner in seven of his next nine seasons.

I was blessed to have both Lemon and Bob Feller on my team—and blessed that I never had to bat against either of them in his prime.

Feller lost the 1947 home opener, 2-0, against Chicago on April 15, but was nothing less than sensational in his next three starts, all of them shutouts.

Bob almost pitched his third career no-hitter, against St. Louis on April 22. There were fewer than 4,000 fans in the stadium because it was so cold, but that also might have been a factor in Feller's success that day. Your hands would sting for 10 minutes when you hit an ordinary fastball on the handle, and Feller's fastball never was just ordinary.

He retired the first 19 batters without giving up anything that would have resembled a base hit.

But then, with one out in the seventh, Al Zarilla spoiled the perfect game with a solid single to center. Neither Joe Gordon nor I, nor center fielder George "Catfish" Metkovich, had a chance for the ball, and Feller wound up with a 5-0, one-hit victory.

Dizzy Dean, the old pitching star of the St. Louis Cardinals, was broadcasting the Browns games that year and said of Feller's one-hitter, "That there is perhaps the best game I ever seen." You didn't need to be a college-educated grammarian to appreciate a great pitching performance.

Feller blanked Hal Newhouser and Detroit, 6-0, in his next start, and pitched a third consecutive shutout—and another one-hitter—to beat Boston, 2-0. There was no suspense in this one as Johnny Pesky got a single in the first inning, but Feller was untouchable the rest of the way.

It was a great way to start the season, and nobody loved it more than Veeck.

We became what I thought were great friends, sometimes too great.

Bill loved to go out after games and drink Burgundy wine— and, sure, to celebrate if we won—but also just to meet people, shake their hands, and sell tickets. He always wanted me to go with him, which I did at the beginning because I thought I should.

But after a little while, only about three weeks, I came to the realization that I couldn't keep up with him, at least not if I planned to continue to play.

With Gordon playing well and two rookies—Eddie Robinson and Dale Mitchell—taking over at first base and left field, we held our own through the first two and a half months. On July 1, our record was exactly even, 28-28.

Unfortunately, the Yankees, with Reynolds becoming one of the league's best pitchers, moved into first place on June 10 and led the rest of the season. Reynolds would go 19-8 and be the Yankees' biggest winner. But I didn't care, and if it bothered Veeck, he never admitted it because we were so happy to have Gordon.

We lost three of our next five and on July 3 fell into fifth place, 10 games behind the Yankees and would not get any closer the rest of the season.

But there was another reason that date—July 3—was significant. It was the day Veeck bought Larry Doby from the Newark Eagles of the Negro National League. Doby would be the American League's first black player, only the second in the major leagues.

We were in Chicago when the news broke. I had been unaware that Veeck had been considering signing a black player.

My first reaction was skepticism. Knowing Veeck as I did, and knowing his penchant for promotion, I immediately wondered if signing a black player was another publicity stunt, a gimmick, another way to sell tickets for a team that apparently was not going to win the pennant again.

He assured me it wasn't. "Larry Doby will be a great player, you'll see," Veeck told me and anybody else who expressed doubts about his motives.

Still, I had to wonder. Veeck said Doby was a second baseman, the position that Joe Gordon was playing—and playing well. Why did we need another second baseman?

"This kid can hit and play anywhere, first base, second base, the outfield, even shortstop," said Veeck, his eyes twinkling as he threw a little barb into me.

"He'll be all yours . . . give him a chance."

I knew it had to be done with care. I couldn't just throw Doby into the lineup anywhere. In fairness to him, I had to pick the right spot, not let the kid get in over his head.

Veeck met with the players before Doby joined us. His words were forceful: "I understand that some of you said if a 'nigger' joins the club, you're leaving. Well, you can leave now because this guy is going to be a bigger star than any guy in this room."

Doby reported two days later, on July 5, at Comiskey Park in Chicago.

Two of our publicity men, Marsh Samuel and Lou Jones, brought Doby downstairs into my office. I greeted him, went over our signals, then walked him through the clubhouse and introduced him to his new teammates.

Most of them were cordial, if not overly friendly. Two players, Eddie Robinson and Les Fleming, refused to shake Doby's hand, but otherwise were not hostile.

Later, Robinson told me that he lived in Baltimore during the off-season and his neighbors would not appreciate his being on the same team as a Negro, but that he himself had nothing against Doby.

Spud Goldstein, our traveling secretary, told me about another incident between Robinson and Doby. I didn't observe it firsthand, but knowing Spud as I did, I have no reason to doubt what he said happened.

I had told Doby to work out at first base. He didn't have a first baseman's glove and asked to borrow Robinson's, but Robinson refused. Goldstein said when he saw what happened, he asked Robinson, "Will you loan your glove to me?" Robinson did, and Goldstein handed the glove to Doby.

Otherwise, to the best of my knowledge, Doby got along okay, though he didn't play much at all that season.

On that first day, after the introductions and our brief team meeting, we trooped through the runway and onto the field. As Doby emerged from the dugout, a few spectators saw him and applauded. Others joined in. It had to be gratifying to Doby.

He and I warmed up together before batting practice. Doby was obviously nervous—and understandably so—but hit pretty well.

He also was noticed very well. Every time he stepped to the plate virtually all the players on the field, including those in the White Sox dugout, stopped what they were doing and paid close attention to the new black kid wearing an Indians uniform for the first time, No. 14.

The fans in the stands watched closely, too, and it's little wonder that Doby felt the pressure of being under a magnifying glass and was uneasy because of it.

Doby's nervousness was even more evident as he took infield practice alongside Gordon at second base. Joe was great with Larry, not just that first day, but every day.

It was especially tough for Doby on the road because, in most cities, he could not stay in the same hotel as the rest of the team, or even eat in the same restaurants. I felt sorry for him, but he handled the situation well, always with Gordon's strong support.

Doby pinch-hit for pitcher Bryan Stephens in his first game with us, July 5. It was against Earl Harrist. We had runners on first and third with one out and were losing, 5-1, in the seventh inning.

I just told him to grab a bat and do his best. I didn't think it was necessary to say anything special. He was a rookie in the American League, but he had been a professional in the Negro League. I realized it was the most pressureful situation he'd ever been in, but that first at-bat had to come sometime, and it was important to do it and get it over with. At least that's the way I felt about it.

I'd also have to say his debut was what you'd call inauspicious. Doby struck out on three pitches. He came back to the dugout with his head down and walked to the end of the bench. If anybody said anything, I didn't hear it, and that was that.

The next day in the *Plain Dealer* Gordon Cobbledick summarized in a column exactly how I felt about Larry. "He will be accepted by his teammates and the customers if he proves to be a good ball player and a good human being, and will be rejected by both if the opposite is true," Cobbledick wrote.

It really was that simple, and Cobbledick proved to be prophetic.

Larry Doby was accepted because he was a good human being and became a good ball player—make that a *very good* ball player.

Some thought had been given to sending Doby out for seasoning, the reasoning being that playing every day in the minors would be good for him. But I figured he'd be better off with us, even if he spent most of the time on our bench.

I always thought I was a pretty good judge of character. I also felt throughout my career that a key to being a good manager was knowing your players, what made them click, what motivated them and what hurt them.

Though I had not been around Doby long, I figured he would be terribly discouraged if we sent him to the minor leagues, but that, if we kept him with us, it would challenge him, which I believe it did.

Doby appeared in 29 games that first season, getting five hits in 32 at-bats for a .156 average, driving in two runs. Though we used him mainly as a pinch-hitter, he played four games at second base, one at first, and one at shortstop, but none in the outfield until 1948, when he would blossom into one of the best and most exciting center fielders in the game.

It was only five days after Doby's debut that the Cleveland Indians were in the headlines again, though this time for a different reason.

Don Black, a 31-year-old right-hander we'd purchased from the Philadelphia Athletics during the winter meetings of 1945— but who also had a drinking problem and was shipped back to the minors in 1946—pitched a no-hitter against his former team on July 10.

Black, who joined Alcoholics Anonymous to salvage his career (though it would be cut short a year later), beat the A's, 3-0, in the first game of a twi-night doubleheader at the stadium. He walked six and struck out five, and what made the no-hitter remarkable is that he survived a third-inning rain delay of 45 minutes that, in many cases, would cause a pitcher to stiffen up and curtail his effectiveness.

It didn't bother Black, though he required a great play by Joe Gordon, two of Ken Keltner's back-handed specialties, and a fine running catch by George Metkovich to preserve the no-hitter, and he went on to post a 10-12 record.

But neither Black's no-hitter, which lifted us one game over .500 into fourth place with a 33-32 record, 10 games behind the Yankees, nor his subsequent performances, nor Doby's presence were enough to boost us back into contention.

The Yankees made a shambles of the pennant race. They took over first place on June 19 and never left it, winning 19 consecutive games in June and July to remove all doubt as to the final result.

It's true, they could not have done it without Reynolds, who would be their ace for six straight seasons, but we still were happy to have Gordon, and would be even happier the following year.

We floundered back and forth between fourth and fifth place the rest of 1947 and finished fourth, 80-74, 17 games behind New York, five behind Detroit, three behind Boston, and two ahead of Philadelphia.

Despite our non-success on the field, the turnstiles clicked merrily all season, and our final attendance—1,521,978—set a Cleveland baseball record for the second consecutive season. More than 27,000 fans turned out for our final game, in which we were shut out, 1-0, by Detroit's Freddie Hutchinson, and Veeck donated the proceeds, $17,551, to the Cleveland Community Chest, a charitable organization.

We had some good individual performances that season: Bob Feller was the only American League pitcher to win 20 games, going 20-11, and his 2.68 earned run average was second in the league, Gordon rebounded to hit .272 with 29 homers and 93 runs batted in, and he and I were selected by the Baseball Writers Association of America as the starting second baseman and shortstop on the major league All-Star team.

Of the 233 writers who participated in the All-Star balloting, 177 voted for me, and 113 for Gordon. My nearest rival was Boston's Johnny Pesky, who was named on 17 ballots. Vernon Stephens of St. Louis did not receive even one vote, the significance of which will become evident later.

Feller also was one of three pitchers picked on the team, along with National Leaguers Warren Spahn of the Boston Braves and Ewell Blackwell of Cincinnati. I hit .307 and was third in the voting for the Most Valuable Player award. It was won by Joe DiMaggio with 202 votes. Ted Williams was second with 201, and I got 168. I also broke my own fielding record for shortstops with a .982 average, making only 14 errors in almost 800 chances.

But I was very disappointed the way we'd finished on the field. I'd felt we were jelling as a team and were ready to make our move, to be a pennant contender.

I knew Veeck was disappointed, too, though he didn't say much when it was all over.

Veeck invited me to attend the World Series with him, but I declined. My contract, the two-year deal I'd signed with Alva Bradley and Roger Peckinpaugh, had expired and I was pretty much in limbo.

Veeck told me to "sit tight," said he'd be "in touch" and went to New York where the Yankees would play the Brooklyn Dodgers in the World Series. I went home to Harvey, Illinois, to my growing family, which then included four—but would be enlarged to five, as Barbara, who was eight, and Sharon, four, were joined by Louis Harry, born October 2, the day of the third game of the World Series. Jim would come along in 1959.

But my relaxation at home didn't last long. While I was sitting tight waiting for Veeck to get in touch, I learned that my managerial and playing careers in Cleveland might be over.

On October 3, the day that Floyd Bevens almost pitched a no-hitter for the Yankees in the fourth game of the World Series, a one-sentence item appeared in a Chicago newspaper. It reported that Veeck was considering trading me to the St. Louis Browns for their shortstop, Vernon Stephens, and several other players.

It turned out that Veeck had told the Cleveland writers—"off the record," of course—that the Browns had proposed the deal because they were unloading all their high-priced players and that he was "only listening" to what Bill DeWitt was offering.

What puzzled me was the part about the Browns wanting to unload their high-priced stars. Sure, Stephens was making good money, but so was I. How could they be expected to cut expenses by trading Stephens for me?

Once the item appeared in the Chicago paper, the Cleveland writers who'd been sworn to secrecy by Veeck were free to report the news, which they did. With a vengeance.

The story broke in Cleveland on October 5 and Veeck flew back from New York to personally explain the situation to the fans. According to the story on the front page of the *Plain Dealer*, Veeck was met at the airport by a crowd of people, some of whom were shouting things like, "Keep Boudreau," and "Trade anybody, but not Boudreau."

Fortunately for me there were a lot of people who thought it was more important to keep me playing for the Indians than it was to satisfy Veeck's craving for a new manager.

The entire scenario was both gratifying and disconcerting. It certainly upset me that Veeck wanted a new manager badly enough to trade me, but it was nice to know that so many of the fans were so vocal in their objection to what Veeck seemed determined to do.

I knew he valued me as a shortstop, but it also had been evident from the day he arrived in Cleveland that he didn't consider me a good manager. When he bought the Indians, according to everything I heard, he favored Jimmy Dykes, though he never admitted it to me.

But now, again according to what people told me, Veeck favored Al Lopez to be the Indians manager. Lopez was the veteran catcher Veeck obtained in a trade with Pittsburgh for Gene Woodling the previous winter. Al caught 61 games for us in 1947, hitting a very respectable .262, but had made it clear at the end of the season that he would retire as a player.

The proposed trade, as it later came out, had me going to St. Louis, along with pitchers Red Embree and Bryan Stephens, for Vernon Stephens, pitcher Jack Kramer, and outfielder Paul Lehner. Veeck also was expected to throw in some cash to sweeten the deal.

Later it was reported that two more players were added to the package, the Indians sending outfielder George Metkovich and the Browns including pitcher Bob Muncrief.

Vernon Stephens, 27 in 1947, had hit .279 with 15 homers and 83 RBI; Lehner, 27, .248; Kramer, 29, had an 11-16 record; and Muncrief, 31, was 8-14. Bryan Stephens, 27, was 5-10; Embree, 30, was 8-10; and Metkovich, 26, hit .254.

I continued to sit tight as Veeck had said, though I was keenly interested in what was happening.

Veeck's response to those who objected to his trading me for Stephens was simply, "Do you really think I, of all people, would want to hurt the Indians? The only thing I want to do is win the pennant."

And to those who speculated that he did not like me personally, Veeck was quoted as saying, "I've never disliked anyone enough to make a move that would hurt my ball club. I'm not mad at Lou at all. If I trade him it will be because I think the deal will make the Indians a better team."

It continued to be a *cause celebre* in Cleveland, with Veeck being deluged with letters—one report placed the total at 4,000—most of them in support of me.

Hal Lebovitz, the baseball writer for the *News*, ran a front-page "Boudreau Ballot" for fans to vote whether to trade or keep me, and kept a daily tabulation of the voting.

Another reporter wrote of the ongoing controversy between Veeck and the fans, "It smashed and splintered and shook the community by its civic heels until all hell popped loose."

Franklin Lewis said in the *Press*, "It is evident that Veeck didn't know Boudreau was immortal in Cleveland. Alva Bradley used to say that he hired the managers of the Indians and the public fired them.

"Boudreau is the one Alva hired—and only an act of God can fire him, apparently."

And Ed McAuley commented in his column in the *News*, "If Veeck were to trade Bob Feller, he might stab some of the fans in their judgments. If he trades Boudreau, he will stab many of the fans in their hearts."

It went on and on for nearly seven weeks and, knowing Veeck as I did, I'm sure he loved it, though I didn't. Finally, on November 17, the Browns made a move that for all practical purposes, ended Veeck's efforts to trade me.

Bill DeWitt, general manager of the Browns, dealt Vernon Stephens and Kramer to Boston for six players and $310,000, which in those days was a huge amount of money.

Veeck, naturally, claimed that the Browns made the deal with the Red Sox only after he bowed to "the will of the fans" and refused to trade me, either to St. Louis or Detroit or Boston or anywhere.

Whatever the truth, I was, and always will be, grateful to the fans in Cleveland for their support of me then and through the years. Every time I've returned to Cleveland for old-timers games or, as I did in 1970 after I was elected to the Hall of Fame and my Indians uniform No. 5 was retired, the fans have been wonderful.

And so it was, after Stephens and Kramer went to Boston, Veeck invited me back to Cleveland, literally and figuratively.

On November 24, Veeck and I met for six and a half hours, from 10:30 a.m. to 5 p.m. I emphasized what I had already made clear to him, that he would have to trade me if he didn't want me to manage, that I would not play for the Indians under another manager.

I also made it clear to him that I wanted another two-year contract, which I had received from Alva Bradley for 1942 and 1943, 1944 and 1945, and 1946 and 1947. "I will not be placed in the position of being on probation," I told him.

By then I had the upper hand, and Veeck agreed. He called the reporters and announced that I had been offered—and had accepted—a new two-year contract to play shortstop for the Indians, and to be their manager through 1949. My salary would be $49,000 each year, $25,000 as manager and $24,000 as a player.

When the reporters questioned the terminology of Veeck's

announcement, he explained that if the Indians traded me to another team, say at the end of the 1948 season, and the other team wanted me only as a player, the Indians would be responsible for the managerial portion of my 1949 salary.

I was pleased the way the *Plain Dealer* reported the contract in its November 25 editions. Bannered across page one was the headline, "BOUDREAU STAYS AS MANAGER 2 YEARS."

And in his story Gordon Cobbledick said:

"Thus ended, apparently in a clear-cut victory for Boudreau, a *cause celebre* that had Cleveland baseball followers in a state of hysteria two months ago when the news leaked out that Veeck was trying to make a trade that would have sent the Indians' spark plug to St. Louis in a deal involving Vernon Stephens, the Browns' shortstop."

Not only did I get what I wanted—especially to stay in Cleveland—I also got assurance of having full authority over the running of the team on the field.

And then, to add frosting on the cake, the Cleveland baseball writers bestowed another honor on me; they named me—by unanimous vote, they said—their "Man of the Year" for 1947.

It is an award given annually to the man who has contributed the most to baseball in Cleveland, and to make it even sweeter, it was one that had been presented to none other than Bill Veeck the previous year.

In their presentation the night of the banquet, the writers sang a parody of the University of Illinois fight song:

"We're loyal to you, Lou Boudreau,
"Our glasses we raise, here's a go,
"We drink to the best, the best in the West,
"And all other points, Lou Boudreau.

"Get in there and fight, Lou Boudreau,
"Our money is down, win, not show,
"But if this is not the year,
"We'll still never shed a tear,
"We're loyal to you, Lou Boudreau."

It was a wonderful climax to a not-so-wonderful year.

And I also would soon discover that it was a prelude to the greatest baseball season of my life—and the greatest season in the baseball history of Cleveland.

A One-Game
Season

Nobody was expecting much from us in 1948, with good reason. We finished fourth in 1947—but Bill Veeck and I were in the minority.

I thought we could win because we were beginning to jell as a team.

Veeck went a step further; he thought we *should* win.

In fact, after everything we'd gone through during the winter, when Veeck was forced to back off in his determination to replace me, I knew we *had* to win or I was finished as a manager of the Indians.

But I also had reached the point where I could have accepted not managing the Indians. It was a concession I was willing to make to the fans of Cleveland, though not to Veeck, which I made clear in my acceptance of the "Man of the Year" award.

"My fondest hope is that when I hang up my spikes for the last time, I will be wearing a Cleveland uniform, either as a manager or player," I said.

It was the "either-as-a-manager-or-player" part that the writers leaped upon after the banquet.

When they asked me to elaborate, I told them, "I meant exactly what I said. Naturally, I'd like to end my days as manager here. But if Bill Veeck decides that he wants someone else to manage the team, I'll gladly step back into the playing ranks. That's what I think of the way the people of Cleveland have treated me. As long as they want to see me play, I'll be happy to play for them, regardless of whether I'm manager or not."

But that didn't lessen the pressure I felt to win the pennant. It was the most intense of my career, more intense even than 1942, when I was the "Boy Manager" of the Indians and everybody thought I was too young and inexperienced to be a major league manager.

It was the pressure that also created the greatest challenge of my career. Nobody wanted to win the pennant more than I, not even Veeck.

And to his credit, Bill did everything possible to help.

I'll admit, I didn't appreciate everything, especially his insistence that I let two of my closest friends, Oscar Melillo and George Susce, go as coaches. It was one of the concessions I had to make to Veeck, though I did so reluctantly. I was determined that if my situation ever changed, I would bring both of them back to the big leagues, which I was able to do later.

Bill McKechnie, "Pops," stayed with me, and my two new coaches also were veterans, Muddy Ruel and Mel Harder.

Ruel previously coached for Jimmy Dykes with the Chicago White Sox, had been an assistant under Commissioner Happy Chandler, and managed the St. Louis Browns in 1947, but was fired after that one season when his team finished last. He was familiar with every aspect of the game.

Harder retired as an active player after his arm trouble in 1947, when he won six games and lost four to become, at that time, the all-time winningest Indians pitcher, with a career record of 223-186. I'll never understand why he has not been voted into the Hall of Fame.

I appreciated having Ruel and Harder on my coaching staff, as I did McKechnie. It's just that I felt bad about losing Melillo and Susce. They helped out in spring training, along with Hall of Famer Tris Speaker, who'd managed the Indians from 1919, when they won their only pennant, through 1926. Speaker had been one of the game's all-time great center fielders and I assigned him to work with Larry Doby, who was being switched from the infield to the outfield. Harder joined McKechnie to speed up the development of Bob Lemon as a pitcher.

Once spring training ended, Melillo and Susce went into scouting, and Speaker returned to retirement, except for special assignments.

Veeck also brought into the fold Hank Greenberg, who would play a prominent role in my future a few years down the road. Greenberg had been one of the game's greatest home run hitters and I had tremendous respect for him as a player.

Veeck had run into Greenberg at Toots Shor's, a famous restaurant in New York, during the 1947 World Series. Greenberg had just finished his thirteenth year in the major leagues and Veeck wanted him to play another season with us, but Greenberg declined. He was 36 and interested only in getting into the business side of baseball.

Veeck apparently wanted Greenberg badly enough that he offered to help Hank buy into the Cleveland club in exchange initially for his services as a consultant and hitting instructor for our young players in spring training.

Greenberg agreed, and so began his new career as Veeck's assistant. He would remain in Cleveland for the next 10 years as a part owner of the Indians and rise to the position of vice president and general manager.

We made a lot of moves that winter, including the release of Al Lopez, who was quickly signed by the Pittsburgh Pirates to manage their Indianapolis farm club in the Class AAA American Association. Veeck helped Lopez land that job, and there was handwriting on the wall, though I wasn't aware of it at the time.

We also picked up some pretty good players—outfielder Wally Judnich and pitcher Bob Muncrief from the St. Louis Browns for $25,000 and three young players who weren't in our plans; infielder Johnny Berardino from the Browns for Catfish Metkovich and $50,000; outfielder Thurman Tucker from the Chicago White Sox for a minor leaguer; reliever Russ Christopher from Philadelphia for $50,000; veteran first baseman Elbie Fletcher, who was signed as a free agent; and outfielder Allie Clark from the Yankees for Red Embree, the pitcher Veeck had wanted to trade for Joe Gordon a year earlier.

Two months into the season we also got outfielder Bob Kennedy from the White Sox for pitcher Al Gettel and outfielder Pat Seerey, and pitcher Sam Zoldak from the Browns for $100,000 and a minor league pitcher.

It was obvious that Veeck felt we needed to strengthen the outfield, which is why he went out and got Judnich, Tucker, Clark, and Kennedy. But that was before McKechnie and I decided to move Larry Doby to the outfield. He started the season in right, with Tucker in center. Eventually, however,

Doby took over in center, and how well he responded is a matter of record. He hit .301 with 14 homers and drove in 66 runs in 1948—and continued to be one of the best center fielders in baseball for the next 12 years .

We also felt it was necessary to improve our pitching, especially the bullpen, and our initial plans were to have rookie Gene Bearden work in relief. Our thinking was that if Bearden could control his knuckleball, it didn't matter that his other pitches were only so-so, which was the reason the Yankees had been willing to trade him.

Our plans also called for Bob Lemon to be a regular starter; he'd earned the opportunity by winning 11 games while losing five primarily as a reliever in 1947, which also proved to be a major decision. Not only did Lemon pitch a no-hitter that season—he beat Detroit, 2-0, on June 30—he went on to win 20 games, and would do so in seven of the next nine seasons.

When you take part in a no-hitter by one of your pitchers, it's something you never forget, especially the key plays. I'll always remember Lemon's for another reason—because it was such an important victory for us. We were in first place, but Philadelphia and New York were breathing on our neck and Boston was right behind them.

Lemon, the former infielder-outfielder who reluctantly switched to pitching, could throw a curveball better than he could hit one. He walked three Tigers that night and was helped by two great fielding plays, one by left fielder Dale Mitchell, who made a sensational running catch to rob George Kell of a hit in the fourth inning, and Ken Keltner, who went behind third base to field a grounder and steal a hit from Hoot Evers in the fifth. Lemon himself gobbled up two grounders in the ninth to cap his no-hitter. It gave him an 11-5 record.

Greenberg got back into uniform in spring training to work with some of our hitters, especially Seerey, who had great power but seldom made contact. Unfortunately, Hank's instructions never took on Seerey, and by June we'd give up on him.

Through it all, as Greenberg worked out with us and took batting practice as part of his work with Seerey, Veeck often "suggested" that Hank should sign a contract and make a comeback. Greenberg just laughed it off until the end of spring training, when he told Veeck he didn't want to play again, that he didn't want to put the uniform on again.

When we broke camp and returned to Cleveland, Greenberg took over the role I had given up the previous season as Veeck's post-game companion. I was glad because I knew Veeck loved to go out after the games and talk, but it had demanded too much of my time because I was still playing.

Greenberg also became Veeck's "morning after" companion and confidant, which didn't particularly please me.

When we were at home, before every game I'd be expected to go upstairs to Veeck's office and discuss my decisions and strategy of the day before with him and Hank. They'd have their scorebooks in front of them and ask what my reasoning was for making certain moves. When we were on the road they'd sometimes—no, make that *often*—call me on the phone and I'd have to explain why I did this or that.

It bothered me, but there wasn't much I could do about it. Veeck was the owner and Greenberg was Bill's right-hand man.

Nothing happened in spring training to dim my optimism for the 1948 season; in fact, I felt more strongly than ever that we could win the pennant. There was no doubt this was the best team I'd had since taking over as manager of the Indians in 1942. My biggest concern was our starting and relief pitching, though I hoped that what we'd seen of Lemon and Bearden in Tucson, Arizona, was not a mirage.

The fellows covering us for Cleveland's three newspapers weren't nearly as optimistic. All three—Gordon Cobbledick of the *Plain Dealer*, Franklin Lewis of the *Press*, and Ed McAuley of the *News*—picked the Yankees to win, with Boston second. Cobbledick and McAuley tabbed us for third and Lewis figured us for fourth.

I predicted in an Indians' publication that we'd finish second, but that was a smoke screen. I didn't want to sound cocky, or put too much pressure on our team. I tried to keep it all on myself.

We opened the season on a high note. Bob Feller pitched a two-hitter to beat St. Louis, 4-0, in front of a mammoth crowd of more than 73,000 fans at Municipal Stadium.

Little did we know that it would be the start of something really great, though it also would be a season of tribulation for Feller, and that the crowd jammed into the stadium would be only the first—and not even the largest—of many more to come.

Doby, who would be a catalyst along with Joe Gordon, Bearden, and Lemon, was our opening-day right fielder, with

Tucker in center. Tucker could outrun Doby, but that was all, and by September, Doby moved into center to stay. It didn't take Bearden that long to earn a shot in the starting rotation, and once he got it, he didn't leave all season.

We went into Washington in early May needing a starter. The Senators' record was poor against left-handed pitchers, but I didn't have one available except for Bearden, who until then had made only a couple appearances in relief.

I thought starting Gene would be a gamble, but it turned out to be no contest. Bearden pitched a three-hitter and had a shutout until the ninth. We beat Washington, 6-1, and from that day—May 8, 1948—Gene Bearden was sensational.

It also was about that point of the season that the wolves started to get on Bob Feller. After beating the Browns on Opening Day, Feller was inconsistent, pitching well one time and poorly the next, and once again the doomsayers came out of the woodwork claiming he was washed up, that he'd been overworked in previous seasons and had lost his fastball.

But I was determined to sink or swim with Feller, and said it publicly. I felt he was only in a slump, and that he'd come around, which he did, though not until later.

The 1948 season wasn't Bob's best—he wound up 19-15 with a 3.56 earned run average and 164 strikeouts in 280 innings—but washed up? That was crazy, and Feller went on to prove it by pitching eight more years in the big leagues. He was remarkable, and, as I've said before, Feller and Bob Lemon were the two best pitchers I ever had.

Feller was famous for his fastball, though it was the curve he developed after returning from the Navy in 1945 that made him so dominant. Lemon had a natural sinker, and the more tired he got, the better his fastball sank.

We went back and forth between first and second place with Philadelphia through the first six weeks of the season, but took over the league lead on May 31 and stayed there for almost two months.

The day before, during a doubleheader in Chicago on May 30, I managed myself into a corner and had to put on the "tools of ignorance" and go behind the plate to catch Russ Christopher.

It happened in the second game, which we won, 13-8, with a nine-run rally in the eighth inning. It was during the rally that I sent a pinch-hitter to the plate for Jim Hegan, and when our second-string catcher, Joe Tipton, got hit with a pitch later that inning, I had nobody else to catch. I got through it okay—one guy stole on me, though I threw another one out—but later Veeck told me if I did it again he'd probably have a heart attack.

I took it to mean he considered me so valuable as a shortstop that he didn't want me to take any chances of getting hurt behind the plate.

We went on to win five straight, as Bearden raised his record to 6-0 on June 8 to boost our lead to three and a half games over Philadelphia and New York, which were tied for second. Except for Feller's ongoing inconsistency, everything was looking good.

Four days later Joe Gordon enjoyed a measure of revenge against his old team by hitting three homers to help us win a doubleheader in Yankee Stadium.

And on June 20—before 82,781 fans at the Stadium, the largest crowd in baseball history until then—Feller and Lemon beat Philadelphia, 4-3 and 10-0, in a double header. Feller's victory raised his record to 6-7.

By July 7, three days after the traditional halfway point, we'd blown our lead and fallen into a virtual tie with the Athletics. We were ahead by three games in the loss column, but they'd won three more. Our record was 44-27, for a .619 percentage, and Philadelphia's was 47-30, .610.

But the big news that day was something else.

Bill Veeck signed Leroy "Satchel" Paige as our second black player and the fourth in baseball history. In addition to Larry Doby, there were Jackie Robinson and Roy Campanella with the Brooklyn Dodgers.

But none of them had the reputation that Paige did—and none of them was even close to Paige in age, though nobody knew exactly how old he was, not even Satch himself, he said.

It set off a storm of controversy. Especially critical of Veeck was the publisher of *The Sporting News*, longtime baseball traditionalist J. G. Taylor Spink.

Spink blasted Veeck in an editorial, calling the signing of Paige nothing more than a blatant publicity stunt, and suggesting that "if Paige were white, he would not have drawn a second thought from Veeck."

The editorial stated: "To bring in a pitching 'rookie' of Paige's age casts a reflection on the entire scheme of operations in the major leagues. To sign a hurler of Paige's age is to demean the standards of baseball in the big circuits."

But I could vouch for Veeck that Spink's charge was not true—and, of course, Veeck soon got the last laugh.

We'd played a night game against Detroit at the stadium on July 5 and it was after two o'clock in the morning by the time I got home. My phone rang early the next day. It was Veeck. He told me, "I'm at the stadium and I have a pitcher I want you to catch and work out and tell me what you think of him."

I told him we had a couple of coaches staying at the Auditorium Hotel, which was close to the Stadium, and asked him to get one of them. He said, "No, I want you to come down and see what I've got here. I want you to work him out and give me your opinion."

What could I do? Veeck was the boss. I said I'd be there in an hour.

It was then I met Satchel Paige for the first time. I'd heard a lot about him when he pitched for the Kansas City Monarchs in the Negro National League, but I never saw him pitch.

We dressed and went out to the field. Hank Greenberg and Abe Saperstein, the owner of the Harlem Globetrotters, were there. So was Gordon Cobbledick, sports editor of the *Plain Dealer*. I guess Cobby had just stumbled onto what we were doing.

I told Satch to loosen up, to run or whatever, and let me know when he was ready. He stuck out his hand, jiggled it, then said, "Mr. Lou," which is what he always called me, "I'm ready. I pitch with my arm, not my legs."

We went to the mound in front of the dugout and threw the ball back and forth about ten minutes. Veeck, Greenberg, Saperstein, and Cobbledick watched but said nothing.

Finally Satch stopped and walked to me. He handed me a folded-up handkerchief, told me to put it on the plate wherever I liked. Inside, outside, middle, wherever.

First I put it on the inside corner. He wound up and threw ten pitches—fast balls and sliders, all with something on them—and nine of them were right over the handkerchief.

He told me to move the handkerchief to the other side of the plate, and he threw ten more pitches the same as before. His fastball had a hop to it, and his slider was tremendous. Seven or eight of his pitches were right over the handkerchief, and those that missed, didn't miss by much.

Then Veeck wanted me to hit against Paige. Emil Bossard, the groundskeeper, set up the batting cage. Paige pitched and I hit some line drives, but not many. He was tough, and I was satisfied. I'd seen enough.

I told Veeck that Paige could help us in the bullpen and as a spot starter. Veeck and Greenberg agreed. We went into the clubhouse and Paige signed a contract.

When the writers asked Paige's age, Veeck said it was 42. Satchel corrected him, saying he was "only about 39." I figured he was closer to 49 or 50.

Satch was a character, once claiming he had pitched 29 consecutive days, and that he was able to do so because he rubbed on his arm a special snake-oil concoction that he got from some Sioux Indians.

He also had an interesting set of rules for, as he said, "staying young." They were:

"Avoid fried meats which angry up the blood; if your stomach disputes you, lie down and pacify it with cool thoughts; keep the juices flowing by jangling around gently as you move; go very light on the vices, such as carrying on in society (because) the social ramble ain't restful; avoid running at all times; and don't look back, something might be gaining on you."

Our only problem with Paige was that it took him so long to warm up we had trouble using him in relief, though that proved to be something of a blessing in disguise. It meant we eventually started him, and the old guy was great.

His first appearance was against the St. Louis Browns in the fifth inning of a game on July 9. By the time he ambled in from the bullpen and reached the mound, eight or nine photographers surged onto the field to take his picture. It was almost a mob scene. Umpire Bill McGowan didn't even try to chase the photographers; he let them snap away as Paige warmed up. Finally, when Satch said he was ready, the photographers left the field and the game resumed.

The first batter Paige faced was Chuck Stevens, who hit the first pitch for a solid single, and you could hear a rustle go through the stands. But Satch got the next three guys and, as he trudged off the field, was given a standing ovation by the 34,780 fans in the stadium that night. The first batter in the sixth also singled, but again Paige retired three in a row.

Old Satch threw everything but the kitchen sink at the Browns, including his famous "hesitation pitch," which none of us had ever seen before. He used a windmill windup and pitched underhand, overhand, and sidearm. The fans booed me when I took him out for a pinch-hitter in the bottom of the sixth.

Paige pitched again in an exhibition game against Brooklyn on July 14, during the All-Star break, and this time a crowd of 64,877 turned out to see what the old geezer had. It was plenty. He held the Dodgers hitless in the seventh and eighth innings, striking out the first three batters he faced, one of them Gil Hodges.

One night later Satch got his first major league victory as we swept a doubleheader in Philadelphia that boosted our lead over the A's to two and a half games. He took over for Bob Lemon in the sixth inning of the second game and gave up a game-tying, two-run homer to Hank Majeski, but then blanked the A's in the final three innings. We won on homers by Ken Keltner in the eighth and Larry Doby in the ninth.

I gave Paige his first start on August 3 and nobody liked it better than Veeck—not even Paige himself. The advance publicity attracted 72,434 fans to the stadium for a game against Washington. It was another record crowd for a Tuesday night game that otherwise would have drawn about 15,000 at best.

Satch was sensational again. He pitched seven strong innings, scattering seven hits and striking out six, and left with a 5-3 lead. Ed Klieman blanked the Senators in the eighth and ninth.

A couple of weeks later, after Paige had pitched a three-hit shutout against Chicago, Veeck fired off a telegram to Spink at the *Sporting News* and, true to form, made the text public. It said: "Paige pitching. No runs, three hits. He definitely is in line for Sporting News' 'Rookie of the Year' award. Regards. Bill Veeck."

Spink didn't appreciate Veeck's humor and retaliated with some harsh words in the following week's *Sporting News*.

But after Paige went 6-1 with a 2.48 earned run average in 21 games that season, Spink published what amounted to a retraction, and even praised Veeck for his good judgment.

It was during Paige's indoctrination that we reached the midway point of the season in first place. It was nothing short of amazing considering that Bob Feller, our acknowledged ace and the game's greatest pitcher, was still struggling and hearing, more now than ever, catcalls from the doomsayers.

Though Feller's record on July 14 was only 9-11, he was picked on the All-Star team along with Bob Lemon, Joe Gordon, Ken Keltner, and me. It was an honor and we all recognized it as such.

I spoke with Veeck about the inclusion of Feller. I knew we couldn't hope to win the pennant without his return to form, and felt four days away from the game would do Feller a lot of good. It also was my opinion that his record did not entitle him to pitch in the All-Star Game, that Bob Lemon, who was 12-7, was more deserving of the honor.

Above all, I didn't want to take the chance of both pitchers being used. Bucky Harris, the manager of the Yankees, a team we were fighting for the pennant, was manager of the American League team.

Veeck agreed, and Feller had no problem with our request that he withdraw.

The way it was handled, however, left Feller wide open to a storm of criticism—unwarranted criticism, I hasten to add—and the way he handled the entire situation intensified the respect I had for him as a man as well as a great pitcher.

Veeck suggested that Feller wrap a bandage around one of his fingers and say he'd cut it doing a household chore. Veeck said that would satisfy the critics.

But Feller wouldn't lie.

So Veeck issued an announcement that Feller had withdrawn for "unknown reasons." It really put Feller under the gun and got the fans in an even greater uproar. They thought Feller had ducked the game again, as he'd been accused of doing in 1947 when he'd hurt his back, a legitimate injury that we tried to keep secret from the rest of the league.

As Ed McAuley wrote in the *News*, "Feller was accused of everything from swell-headedness to running out on the players' pension fund," which then was the primary recipient of the game's proceeds. "One colleague (fellow sportswriter) simply refused to believe the truth. 'If Veeck is taking the rap now,' he insisted, 'he's just covering up for Feller. Bob is so hungry for headlines that he knew he'd get more publicity if he didn't pitch than if he did.'"

Veeck eventually issued a retraction. "Bucky Harris would be perfectly within his rights if he used both Feller and Lemon in the All-Star Game. We're perfectly within our rights when we make it impossible for him to do so. We're fighting for the pennant, and we're not taking any risk of having our two best pitchers used two days before we open one of the most important series of the season (in Philadelphia)," Veeck was quoted in the papers.

It was well said, but did no good for Feller, and he was the target of unfair abuse the rest of the season simply because he had obeyed orders.

The American League won the All-Star Game, 5-2. Joe Gordon and I both went 0-for-2, but Ken Keltner played the whole game at third base and singled and scored a run in three trips to the plate. Bob Lemon didn't see any action, which disappointed him, but not me. We needed a strong Lemon and a comeback by Feller in the second half to keep our hold on first place, which by then had shrunk to a half game over Philadelphia.

But with Paige pitching as well as he was, I told the writers, knowing that our players would read it, that I believed we would win the pennant. "We're as good as anybody," I said. "We've stayed up there without Feller at his best, and I still think he will come around, and that we will win."

My analysis was: "The Athletics have good pitching but just fair hitting. The Yankees can't win without Joe DiMaggio in good shape and at his best, which he isn't. The Red Sox are the main danger, but they will be on the road most of September. Besides, I think we can beat them in their park with our right-handed power."

But as they say, actions speak louder than words, and I was fortunate enough to make my point loud and clear on August 8.

We'd beaten New York the day before for our sixth straight victory, and three of us—the Indians, Yankees, and Athletics—were in a virtual tie for first place, separated by only .002 percentage point. Our record was 58-39, New York's was 59-40, and Philadelphia's was 61-42.

It was a Sunday doubleheader and 73,484 fans were in the stands hoping to see us extend our winning streak. I was unable to play for the second straight day and managed the team from the bench. I had an assortment of injuries from a collision three

The 1933 Thornton High School basketball team—state champions. That's me sitting third from the left.

At the University of Illinois, my teammates often referred to me as the "Flying Frenchman." Here I am with head basketball coach Doug Mills during my junior year when I was team captain.

Another happy day in my baseball career as I sign a contract with team president Bill Veeck looking on.

With Tris Speaker, Hank Greenberg, and Bob Hope.   Hope grew up in Cleveland and was a minority stockholder of the Indians.

Joe DiMaggio was the best right-handed hitter I ever played with or against.

Our great 1948 Cleveland Indians team, World Series Champions. That's me in the front row sitting next to Bill Veeck.

Here I am at a WGN pre-sentation with Ernie "Mr. Cub" Banks and (standing from left) Jack Brickhouse, John Domeier, and Ward Quaal.

Having a postgame talk with one of the best pitchers in the game, Bob Lemon (right), after a 9-0 victory over Boston.

Bob Feller (left) and Ken Keltner (right) after we beat Boston to put us in a first-place tie with the Red Sox during the 1948 season.

Red Sox manager Joe Cronin and I have a chat with baseball immortal Babe Ruth.

Della, Bill Veeck, and I enjoying the 1948 Championship parade.

I gave the ageless and legendary Satchel Paige his first major league start in 1948.

The 1948 American League's Most Valuable Player award is one of my most treasured honors.

Our basement in Dolton, Illinois, full of memorabilia from my career.

Officiating a pregame ceremony at Wrigley Field, I met with the umpire crew and Mets manager Casey Stengel.

"Hamming it up" in the broadcast booth—or should I say "salami"-ing it up.

LOUIS BOUDREAU
"Lou"

Shortstop
Bats: Right   Throws: Right
Ht: 5'11"   Wt: 185 lbs.
Born: Harvey, Illinios 7/17/17

Playing Record
1938-1950 Cleveland Indians
1951-1952 Boston Red Sox

Games	1646	Triples	66
At Bats	6030	Home Runs	68
Runs	861	Runs Batted In	789
Hits	1779	Batting Average	.295
Doubles	385		

Hall of Fame

INDUCTION DAY
July 27, 1970
Cooperstown, New York

Courtesy of Lou Boudreau

My Hall of Fame "scorecard."

Courtesy of Lou Boudreau

The culmination of my career—receiving my Hall of Fame plaque in 1970 from Commissioner Bowie Kuhn. It's the greatest honor any player can hope to receive.

With Senior Associate
Athletic Director Bob
Todd as my University
of Illinois number is
retired in 1992.

Surrounded by my family,
(from top clockwise)
Della, Barbara, Jim, Lou
Jr., and Sharon.

days earlier with Washington's Gil Coan. He slid into me hard trying to steal second base and I wound up with a contusion of my right shoulder, a bruised right knee, a very sore right thumb, and a sprained left ankle.

I wasn't even wearing a shoe on my left foot, which I soaked in a bucket of ice water during the game; my back and thumb were taped up, and I had a brace on my knee. Johnny Berardino played shortstop in my absence.

Sam Zoldak, the left-handed pitcher we acquired from St. Louis in the middle of June, started but was knocked out. We were losing the opener, 6-1, in the seventh inning, and were in deep trouble the way Spec Shea was pitching for the Yankees.

But Ken Keltner walked, and after Shea got the second out, Berardino homered into the left-field stands. Eddie Robinson followed with another homer and we were only two runs behind. Jim Hegan kept the rally alive with a single, Allie Clark walked, and Dale Mitchell also singled to load the bases.

Bucky Harris came out of the Yankees dugout to talk to Shea. With Thurman Tucker, a left-handed hitter due next, he brought in Joe Page, their ace left-handed reliever. I'm sure Bucky figured I couldn't hit because I was hurt, and knew the only other right-handed batters we had on the bench were Joe Tipton and Bob Kennedy.

I looked at Lefty Weisman, our trainer, and asked him what he thought. Should I bat for Tucker? Lefty said no, that if I reinjured myself, I'd miss a lot more time.

But I felt this might be our last shot, and also—however immodest it sounds—I knew I was the best we had available.

While Page warmed up, I put on my sock and shoe and went to the bat rack. Nobody said anything, though I remember seeing Bill McKechnie nod his head and smile.

When I stepped out of the dugout with a bat in my hand, and field announcer Jack Cressen intoned, "Attention please, batting for Tucker, No. 5, Lou Boudreau," the fans went crazy. Their cheers were deafening and sent a chill up my spine. I forgot about how badly my ankle hurt, or that my back was stiff, or that my thumb was so sore.

Page's first pitch was a ball. I fouled off his second. His third pitch was inside for ball two, and then umpire Art Passarella called Page's fourth pitch a strike. I didn't like it and told Passarella.

Now, with the count 2-and-2, the crowd was hushed, expectant, probably fearing the worst.

I figured Page would come in with another fastball. He did and I was ready for it. I hit a line drive to the right of second base into right-center field. It might have been a double, but I barely made it to first base, my ankle and back hurt so much.

It brought two runs home, tying the score.

The ovation I got as I limped off the field was even greater than the one I got when I was announced as a pinch-hitter. It was one of the highlights of my career, second only to winning the playoff game—and we never would have gotten to the playoff if we hadn't beaten the Yankees that day.

Later I heard from Gordon Cobbledick that Veeck had said in the press box, "Even if Boudreau doesn't get a hit, this is the most courageous thing I've ever seen in baseball."

Whether it was courageous or ill-advised, as Weisman had suggested, I felt I had to do it. I also believe that putting myself on the spot as I did drove home a point that I'd always tried to make, that I would never ask any of my players to do anything I was unwilling to do myself.

We won that game, 8-6, when Robinson hit another home run in the eighth inning, and went on to sweep the doubleheader.

We clung to first place for the next two weeks with Bearden, Lemon, and Paige continuing to pitch well, though Feller was still struggling. He failed to go the distance in seven consecutive starts after the All-Star break, though I refused to give up on him. As I'd said earlier, we would sink or swim with Bob, and I was determined to do so.

We went into Boston and lost on a ninth-inning home run by none other than Vernon Stephens. It dropped us into second place, one-half game behind the Red Sox, and only one and a half ahead of New York.

By Labor Day, September 6—the day baseball traditionalists say the team that's in first place will win the pennant—we were third, four and a half games behind Boston and three behind New York. It did not look good.

Veeck was quoted in the *Press*, "There's not much chance left now . . . it will take a miracle for us to win."

I couldn't argue with him, though I wished he hadn't said it publicly.

Then we lost Don Black, who had done so well in his battle against alcoholism. Black suffered a brain hemorrhage while batting in a game against St. Louis on September 13. He survived, though he never pitched again.

But we didn't give up, and neither did the fans.

Six days after Black was stricken, a crowd of 75,382 turned out to see us sweep a doubleheader from Philadelphia. Veeck loved it for two reasons: it boosted us back into second place, a half game behind Boston, and also, the crowd set a season attendance record of over 2,300,000, and we still had four home dates left. We'd finish with a final total of 2,620,627.

Feller finally showed signs of regaining his stuff by pitching a three-hitter to beat the Red Sox, 5-2, on September 22 in front of 76,772 fans in a benefit game for Black. It was originally scheduled for the afternoon, but Veeck got permission to change it to a night game over the heated objection of Boston manager Joe McCarthy. He wanted to face Feller in the daylight, not at night, and also accused Veeck of doing it to generate greater fan support, which it did, of course.

There was a World Series atmosphere and Feller responded with one of his best performances of the season, and we climbed into a tie for first place with the Red Sox. It also raised over $40,000 for Black and his family.

We lost the next day to Detroit, while New York was beating Boston, throwing the three of us into a tie with seven games left. I thought the schedule favored us because the Red Sox and Yankees would end the season playing each other twice in Boston.

How wrong I was, thanks to Hal Newhouser, our old nemesis with Detroit. But first Bearden and Feller each came through again against Chicago, while Washington was beating Boston twice, and Philadelphia knocked off New York twice. It put us back on top by two games with three to play against the Tigers.

We lost the first, 5-3, as Detroit rallied for three runs in the ninth inning off Lemon, who failed for the fourth straight time to win his twenty-first game. That left us with a one-game lead over the Red Sox and Yankees.

I kept the reporters out of the clubhouse after the game; I wanted to make sure nobody made any negative comments in the papers, though I met with the writers in the press room. I told them I felt we were still in the driver's seat, but that we couldn't relax, we had to keep plugging away and not count on the Yankees knocking off the Red Sox, or vice versa.

This time I proved to be right.

Bearden beat the Tigers, 8-0, for his nineteenth victory on October 2 to clinch a tie for the pennant, while the Red Sox were beating the Yankees, 5-1.

Now all we had to do was win our last game, or for the Yankees to beat the Red Sox, and Cleveland would have its first pennant in 28 years.

But we didn't win—and neither did the Yankees.

In what was expected to be another classic duel between Feller and Newhouser, the Tigers had an easy time of it, beating us, 7-1. Newhouser, starting with only three days' rest, pitched as though he were trying to win the pennant for Detroit. He held us to five hits while Feller was knocked out in the third inning when the Tigers scored four runs. We never got close.

All that was left for us was to sit in our clubhouse and hope for the best, that the Yankees would win the pennant for us.

They didn't. An hour or so later we got the news from Boston. The Red Sox beat the Yankees, 10-5, pulling them into a tie with us, each with a 96-58 record.

And because we'd lost a coin toss two weeks earlier when the possibility of a tie became evident, we had to go to Boston the next afternoon for the first playoff for a pennant in major league history.

Just like that it had become a one-game season—October 4— with the winner to open the World Series against the Braves in Boston on October 6. I told the players, "What the hell, we were planning to go to Boston anyway. All this means is that now we have to go to Fenway Park first, a day early. It's that simple."

I repeated the same story to the reporters. I had to say something.

What I didn't stress, because there already was enough pressure, was that this would be the most important game of baseball most of us, if not *everybody*, would ever play. Certainly, it was for me.

The Red Sox were immediately installed as favorites, and understandably so, I should say. The game would be played in Fenway Park, where the Red Sox are always dangerous because their teams are tailored to take advantage of the "Green Monster." The wall in left field is only 315 feet from the plate, much like League Park was structured, except that its short field was in right.

Another and probably better reason the "smart money" was on the Red Sox was the way we ended the regular season. Instead of finishing strong to climb into first place, we had faltered and slid downhill into the tie. We'd lost our momentum by losing four of our last 10 games, and two of three. The defeat by Newhouser and the Tigers on the final day was especially demoralizing.

Nobody—not the gamblers or the writers or the fans or even Bill Veeck—had to tell me that our backs were against the wall, that our chances were not good.

But I refused to admit it to anybody, especially not to my team.

The immediate speculation, of course, concerned my choice of a starting pitcher in the playoff game.

I told the players that because it meant as much to them as it did to me, I wanted everybody to have some input as to which pitcher we should start. Nobody volunteered, so I said my choice was Gene Bearden.

There were a few oohs and aahs, but that's all.

I acknowledged that Bearden had pitched the day before and would be working with only two days' rest, but that he was the best we had at that time, better than Feller, better than Lemon, and better than Steve Gromek.

I also told them what Casey Stengel had always told me about Bearden, that if he threw strikes with his knuckleball, he could beat anybody—and Bearden had been throwing strikes.

Besides, we'd have everybody in the bullpen from the start, including Feller and Lemon, in case Bearden got in trouble.

The only one who didn't like my idea was Johnny Berardino. "You can't pitch a left-hander in Fenway Park," he said.

We talked about it some more. For about 10 minutes. Then— and I'll never forget this—Joe Gordon stood up and said, "Lou, we went along with your choice for 154 games and finished in a tie. There's not a man in this room who, two weeks ago, wouldn't have settled for a tie. I'm sure we can go along with you for another game."

It was gratifying to hear, coming as it did from one of the greatest players in the game.

And with that, Berardino said, "I'll go along," and it was settled. Our pitcher would be Gene Bearden.

But I wasn't finished. "One thing I want to do, and I want everybody to go along with me on this," I said. "I want to keep our decision to start Bearden a secret. I don't want the Red Sox, or anybody, to know our plan."

My reasoning was that everybody, especially the reporters, would guess our pitcher would be Lemon or Feller. "Let them think so," I said. "Let them bother Lemon and Feller on the train all night, that way they'll leave Bearden alone and he'll get some rest."

Which is the way we did it. I was told later that Lemon and Feller were being interviewed at their berths most of the night, and both of them maintained that I had not made a decision.

Feller, Lemon, and Bearden—*especially Bearden*—handled it well. Feller and Lemon understood and agreed with my reasoning.

And Bearden, who had all the pressure on his shoulders, was remarkable. His attitude probably was best summarized when I talked to the team about catcher Jim Hegan's signs. Knowing that Bearden would throw knuckleballs four out of five pitches, I said Hegan would change signs if Bearden got knocked out of the box.

Bearden was insulted. "What the hell do you mean?" he demanded. "There isn't going to be any change of pitchers."

He was an amazing person. A tough guy, a good guy to have on your side. He liked to be in the limelight with pressure on him. He handled it so well, maybe because he'd seen so much action in the Navy during the war. Nothing on a baseball field ever bothered Gene Bearden. At least he never seemed to show it.

When we got to Fenway Park, I did what I usually had done— only this time I did more of it.

I always put a ball in the locker and under the cap of the pitcher who was to be our starter that game. This time I put a ball under Lemon's cap, another one under Feller's cap, and one under Bearden's cap.

I knew Johnny Orlando, who was then the visiting-team clubhouse attendant, would tell the Red Sox who we were going to pitch, and I didn't want them to know until the last minute.

The funny thing is, I didn't believe them when Joe McCarthy told reporters he was going to start Denny Galehouse against us. I was sure he'd have somebody else warming up where we couldn't see him.

McCarthy previously had announced that his pitcher would be Ellis Kinder or Mel Parnell, though we knew he also had Jack Kramer as well as Galehouse. All were right-handers except Parnell. Kramer had won 18 games, Parnell 15, Kinder 10 and Galehouse eight. Joe Dobson, an old teammate of ours, won 16 that season, including the victory over New York the day before, forcing the playoff.

Galehouse had pitched well against us in relief earlier in the season, shutting us out on two hits for eight innings, which probably was the reason McCarthy chose him to start. Still, right up until the time Galehouse took the mound, I expected somebody else. For that reason I had Spud Goldstein, our traveling secretary, wander around Fenway Park where the Red Sox had workout areas, looking for one of their pitchers warming up.

About 10 minutes before game time, and while I could still change our lineup, Spud reported that he couldn't find a trace of anybody.

It meant Galehouse would at least be the Red Sox starter.

Despite Galehouse being right-handed, I decided to pack our lineup with as much right-handed power as possible. It led to a decision that I later learned was second-guessed by Bill Veeck and Hank Greenberg, who also had questioned the wisdom of pitching Bearden in Fenway Park.

I started Bob Kennedy in right field and put Allie Clark, an outfielder, at first base. The only left-handed batter in the lineup was left fielder Dale Mitchell, who'd hit .336 as our leadoff batter. I was aware that Clark had never played first base in the big leagues, but I wanted him to get at least two pops at the "Green Monster," and then we'd get regular first baseman Eddie Robinson into the game.

I explained to Robinson why I was playing Clark, and tried to assure him it was not a reflection on him. Eddie was hurt, but didn't make waves.

Neither did Veeck and Greenberg, though they probably wanted to. They came down to the dugout before the game and we talked. They did not say much, at least to my face, except to wish us good luck.

But in Greenberg's book, *The Story of My Life*, published after his death in 1986, he said of my decisions to start Bearden and Clark, "You can imagine Bill Veeck's shock. I had to agree with him. It was a daring move. It took a lot of guts."

I never disputed that it took a lot of guts. But I did what I thought was best. I learned a lot earlier that managing a major league team is not an easy job, that it often takes courage - okay, a *lot of guts*—to stick to your convictions, to do what you think is right, without worrying about being second-guessed, even by your bosses.

Besides, I knew I was under the gun. I knew how important it was for us to win, and I'd made up my mind that if we got beat, it was going to be with what I thought was my best shot.

Fenway Park is not very large, but the capacity crowd of nearly 34,000 sounded like twice as many the way the fans roared when the Red Sox took the field.

Galehouse responded by getting the first two batters, Mitchell on a fly to Ted Williams in left field, and Clark on a grounder to third baseman Johnny Pesky. Then it was my turn and the adrenaline was really flowing.

I went to the plate the same as I always did. I concentrated on the pitcher and the strike zone. I was not a "guess hitter," though I did look for certain pitches in certain situations. And I never tried to hit a home run, only to make contact.

Galehouse's first two pitches were balls. I fouled off the next one, then hit a fastball to left. In Cleveland it would have been an out. But we were in Fenway Park and the ball soared into the netting over the "Green Monster," my seventeenth—but not last—homer of the season.

I'd have to call it the biggest hit of my career, even bigger than my bases-loaded single off Joe Page on August 8, when we rallied to win a doubleheader, because this one meant so much more.

When I returned to the dugout I could sense a difference in our guys. The tightness was gone, the looseness that had characterized our team most of the season was back.

The Red Sox retaliated in their half of the first as Pesky doubled with one out, took third as Williams grounded out, and scored on a single by Vernon Stephens (yes, again *that* Vernon Stephens).

I can't say I second-guessed my decision to start Bearden, but I admit, I began to feel some concern about Gene. We all did, but shouldn't have.

Bearden checked the Red Sox the next three innings and I led off the fourth with a single. I took second on a single by Gordon and was immediately confronted with another major decision that I figured would be faulted by Veeck and Greenberg.

But again, I did what I thought was best. "Always let the hitters hit," Casey Stengel advised me once, and since Ken Keltner was a hitter, I let him hit instead of ordering the orthodox strategy, a sacrifice bunt.

Keltner hit the ball over the screen atop the "Green Monster" for his thirty-first homer, and we were on our way to the World Series with a 4-1 lead.

Now, for sure, the tightness was gone. It was all on the Red Sox.

Keltner's homer finished Galehouse, and Ellis Kinder couldn't stop us either. We got another run as Larry Doby doubled and came around on a sacrifice bunt and an infield out for a 5-1 lead.

It got even better in the fifth when I hit another homer, my eighteenth, for a five-run cushion that was more than enough for Bearden. The Red Sox scored twice in the sixth on Bobby Doerr's homer, but we got them back in the eighth and ninth.

When I came to bat in the ninth the fans gave me a standing ovation, even though most of them were for the Red Sox. It provided me with another memory I'll forever cherish, and then I singled again, going 4-for-4, and we won, 8-3.

When Bearden got Birdie Tebbetts to ground out to Keltner to end the game, I rushed to the box alongside our dugout where Della was sitting and hugged her. "We made it! We made it! We made it!" was all I could say. She was crying. I was never so happy.

Somebody else who was thrilled by our victory was Mrs. George A. Martin, the widow of the man who'd convinced the other 11 members of the Indians' board of directors to hire me to manage the Indians in 1942.

I received a telegram from her that said, "My hearty congratulations to you and your team over your splendid finish. Mr. Martin would have been proud of his boys and their manager."

It was the greatest sense of excitement, of achievement, of pride I'd ever felt.

Bearden had been magnificent, allowing only five hits and striking out six for his twentieth victory. Except in the first inning, he never faltered, and when the game ended, he was carried off the field.

Veeck also had tears in his eyes as he hobbled over to join the celebration. He threw his arms around me and all he could say was, "Thanks. Just thanks."

Later Bill paid me the supreme compliment.

Nothing could have pleased me more than when he told the press, "We didn't win the pennant in 1948 . . . we won it on November 25, 1947, the day I rehired Lou Boudreau."

Who Could
Ask For More?

It had been a great season, the most thrilling in Cleveland baseball history and certainly one of the greatest that any team could hope to have.

A lot of people thought the World Series would be anticlimactic for us, considering how hard we'd fought to get there, and also because of our victory party after we beat the Red Sox for the pennant. It was wild, but *wonderfully* wild, and nobody celebrated more than Bill Veeck.

I was determined to prevent a letdown and reminded everybody that we hadn't reached our final objective. I was counting especially on the guys who'd got us where we were, to take us a step further.

Gene Bearden and Bob Lemon were magnificent, each of them winning 20 games, and Bob Feller, who struggled but never gave up, finished strong with seven consecutive victories before losing the final game of the regular season.

We couldn't have done it without the leadership on and off the field of Joe Gordon, who hit .280 with 32 homers and 124 runs batted in, or Ken Keltner, whose numbers were even better, a .297 average, 31 homers and 119 RBIs.

Dale Mitchell, who hit .336, was the triggerman as our leadoff batter, and the emergence of Larry Doby offered more proof that Bill Veeck was an astute judge of baseball talent.

Doby was an introverted and sensitive youngster when he joined us out of the Negro National League in July 1947, but in

1948 he blossomed into one of baseball's best players, serving notice with a .301 average and 14 homers that he would soon be one of the game's brightest stars.

It also was another good season for me, certainly my best from a statistical standpoint. I hit .355, second in the American League to Ted Williams's .369, drove in 106 runs—both career highs—and struck out only nine times in 560 at-bats.

I would be voted the Most Valuable Player that winter, and I honestly don't think any man in any sport had as great a year as I did in 1948, which I say with pride, not boastfulness. I was motivated by Veeck's low regard for me as a manager, and inspired by the fans of Cleveland, who supported me when he tried to trade me to St. Louis.

It was during the victory party, before Della and I got away to let the fellows have their fun, that Gordon grabbed a microphone and made a little speech. I remember his words very well. Fact is, I'll never forget them.

"As the player representative," he said, "I've been asked to propose a toast, and here it is. Let's all drink to the greatest major leaguer in the business, Lou Boudreau."

I was overwhelmed, especially that it was Gordon who paid me such a wonderful tribute.

The gratification I felt for the success we'd enjoyed ran through my mind the morning after we'd beaten the Red Sox, which also was the "morning after" of another sort—probably the greatest party any team could have to celebrate winning the pennant.

Oh, what a sorry-looking bunch of hung over but happy players reported to the visiting team's clubhouse at Braves Field in Boston on October 5, the day before we would open the World Series against the National League champion Braves.

Despite his second-guessing my choice of Bearden to pitch and Allie Clark to play first base in the playoff game, Veeck had hoped for (if not expected) the best, and had everything ready for a celebration in the Kenmore Hotel after the game.

I told the players to have fun, to enjoy the party because, as the good Lord knew, they'd earned it.

But I also told them that, while all my rules were suspended for the night, they'd be back in place the next day, and anybody who missed our 10 a.m. workout would be fined $250.

We didn't do anything more than suit up and loosen up. We did some running, but no hitting. To be honest, I was afraid—considering the condition of some of the fellows—that somebody would get hurt. It was so bad, in fact, that Lefty Weisman, our trainer, passed out numbers for the guys to get into the whirlpool to soak away the champagne they'd poured into themselves.

Bearden probably was in the worst shape, but nobody could blame him, considering the job he'd done all season, especially in the playoffs.

I counted on everybody being ready to go by game time the next day, when Feller would take the mound against Johnny Sain, who'd won the most games in the major leagues that season, 24, while losing 15. It turned out that Bob would pitch one of his finest games—but also would suffer one of the cruelest twists of fate.

The two ace pitchers were deadlocked in a scoreless duel for seven innings, neither giving an inch in front of a crowd of more than 40,000 screaming fans who were even more eager for the Braves to win since our victory over the Red Sox.

Feller had a one-hitter going; he'd allowed only a fifth inning single by Marv Rickert. Ironically, Rickert was playing only because our former teammate—and Feller's former roommate—Jeff Heath, had suffered a broken ankle sliding into home plate with five games left in the Braves' season.

It had to be very frustrating for Heath, who finally was living up to the great potential predicted of him before he was traded to Washington in the winter of 1945-46. Heath hit .319 with 20 homers for the Braves before breaking his ankle in 1948, and would retire in 1949 after an unsuccessful comeback attempt.

Sain was working on a four-hitter and retired us in order in the top of the eighth, setting the stage for Feller to make a critical mistake—which set up an even more critical mistake by National League umpire Bill Stewart.

But then, I probably was guilty of one, too.

Feller walked Bill Salkeld, the Braves catcher, on a 3-and-2 pitch to lead off the bottom of the eighth. Phil Masi, their other catcher, ran for Salkeld and was bunted to second. I told Feller to intentionally walk the next batter, Eddie Stanky, to set up a double play, since Sain was the next batter. Feller tried to talk me out of it, but I insisted.

I was widely second-guessed for my decision to walk Stanky, but if I had it to do over again, I wouldn't change a thing.

You might remember that Branch Rickey once said about Stanky, "He can't hit, he can't run, he can't throw, and he can't field—all he can do is beat you," and I wasn't about to let him beat us.

Feller walked Stanky, but Sain, instead of grounding out, flied out. That brought up Tommy Holmes, who was one of the National League's best hitters. He batted .325 that season.

The go-ahead run was on second and, with a dangerous hitter at the plate, the situation was perfect for the pickoff play I'd designed for our pitchers. It was mainly to hold a runner close to second base, to prevent him from scoring on a single, although, if we picked him off, that would be even better, especially in this case.

I really believe our pickoff play saved us 18 to 20 runs in 1948 because, once we showed it, many base runners were intimidated by the *possibility* that we'd use it.

With Holmes at bat, I played right behind Masi as he led off from second. I gave the pickoff sign by holding my glove over my left knee. Normally a shortstop never stands in his fielding position with his glove over his knee; it's always off his knee with the fingers and the palm down, ready for the ball to be hit to him.

In order to work, the play depended on perfect timing between the pitcher and shortstop.

I also had a sign for Larry Doby in center field for him to back me up in case the pitcher's throw is wild. When I raised the heel of my right foot, Doby would know the pickoff was on and come racing in toward the infield as the pitcher wheeled to throw.

As soon as Feller saw me give the sign, he was to turn his head directly to the batter and start counting—*one-thousand one, one-thousand two*—and then wheel and fire the ball to second base.

As soon as Feller turned his head to the batter and I saw the back of his head, I was to break for second base, which gave me a one-step head start on the runner.

Everything worked perfectly. Feller's throw was right there and I tagged Masi as he dived back into the base. I got him from his elbow up to his shoulder. There was no doubt about it in my mind. It wasn't even close. We got Masi and the inning was over.

But not in Stewart's eyes. At least not *then*.

The umpire called Masi safe. He said I tagged Masi "high," after his right hand reached the base. But photographs of the play showed that Masi's hand was still several inches from the base while I was putting the tag on his upper arm. But by then it didn't matter.

I argued with Stewart. So did Feller and Joe Gordon, but to no avail.

My mistake probably was that I didn't alert Stewart and the rest of the umpires in the managers' meetings with them prior to the series. The reason I didn't was that Billy Southworth of the Braves was in the room at the time. I should have called the umpires aside and told them to be ready for our pickoff, but I didn't.

For years thereafter Stewart stuck to his guns, never admitting that he had blown the call.

Also later, whenever Masi and I would cross paths on the banquet circuit or at old-timers games, he steadfastly insisted that he was safe, that Stewart had called the play right—until after Stewart passed away. Then Masi admitted to me that he was out.

After Stewart blew the call on Masi, Feller went after Holmes with a fastball. He got it a little high and Holmes, swinging late, slashed a line drive just inside the third-base line past Ken Keltner. It scored Masi, of course, and that was the game, though we mounted a mild threat in the ninth.

I flied out and Joe Gordon fouled out. Our hopes stayed alive as Ken Keltner reached on an error, but Walt Judnich was called out on strikes to end it.

It was a heartbreaking loss for Feller, and would continue to be frustrating over the years. In 18 seasons in the major leagues virtually the only achievement escaping Feller, the greatest pitcher of our time, was winning a World Series game.

We won the next three games, and if there is such a thing as poetic justice—though it was small consolation—it occurred during Bob Lemon's 4-1 victory over the Braves and Warren Spahn the next afternoon.

We pulled the play again in the first inning, when Lemon was struggling. The Braves already had scored one run and had two runners aboard with one out. Lemon picked Earl Torgeson off second. This time American League umpire Bill Grieve was there to make the call and I've got to believe it was a matter of his being more alert to the possibility that we'd try the play because of what happened the day before.

After Lemon got Torgeson, he struck out Rickert to end the rally, the inning and, as it turned out, the Braves' scoring. We took a 2-1 lead in the fourth on my double and singles by Joe Gordon and Larry Doby, and Lemon went all the way, scattering eight hits.

That sent us back to Cleveland for the third game, and it seemed the entire city was going wild over us—though it would turn out to be mild compared to the celebration that would follow four days later.

Gene Bearden, the rookie who deserved most of the credit for our being in the World Series, pitched the third game in front of 70,306 roaring fans at the stadium. He was masterful—make that *sensational*—again by shutting out the Braves, 2-0, on five hits. Gene faced only 29 batters and, what's more, got two of our five hits himself, including a double that resulted in our first run in the third inning.

Because we had a 2-1 lead in games and were at home for two more, I decided to gamble for the fourth game. I started Steve Gromek, a side-arming right-hander who'd won nine and lost three as a spot starter that season. I considered coming back with Feller with three days' rest, but felt an extra day would be good for him. Besides, if Gromek could beat Sain and the Braves, we'd be in terrific shape.

That's what Gromek did, in front of an even larger crowd, 81,897 fans who went absolutely bonkers for us. You can say what you will, but even so-called "hardened" professionals respond to the cheers of a crowd, which our players did for the fans in the stadium that day.

I did, too, driving in our first run in the first inning with a double after Dale Mitchell led off with a single. I tried to stretch my hit into a triple and, the truth be told, I think I did, though the umpire—none other than our friend from the first game, Bill Stewart—said I didn't.

Larry Doby homered in the third and Gromek extended the Braves' shutout streak to 23 innings before yielding a solo homer to Marv Rickert in the seventh. I kept the bullpen ready, but Gromek didn't need help. Steve struck out two of the last three batters for a 2-1 victory, and we were riding high with Feller set to go the next day.

By then the fans were almost fanatical in their zeal and 86,288 of them, a record that still has not been surpassed, were on hand to see us win the Indians' second world championship, and Feller his first World Series game.

But we all were disappointed, especially Feller.

Feller had nothing. He was hammered for two homers by Bob Elliott in the first and third innings, and though we battled back to take a 5-4 lead in the fourth, October 10, 1948 was not our day.

Bill Salkeld homered off Feller to tie the score in the sixth, and all hell broke loose in the seventh. Two hits around a sacrifice bunt put the Braves on top, 6-5. In retrospect, I know I went too far with Feller but I wanted to see him get a World Series victory, considering all he had done over the years for the Cleveland club.

But when he gave up the lead in the seventh, I brought in Ed Klieman and things went from bad to worse. Before the inning was over the Braves scored six times and won, 11-5.

The only good thing that happened was that Satchel Paige, the ageless black star who never got a chance to show what he could do in the major leagues until his career was nearly over, made his first and only appearance in a World Series game. He pitched to two batters in the seventh and retired both of them.

I know Satch was disappointed that he didn't start a World Series game. He got the ear of a sportswriter in New York and it was written that he expected to pitch one of the games. But there was no way I could use him ahead of my "Big Three" of Bearden, Feller, and Lemon, or even ahead of Gromek.

Suddenly everything was not so comfortable after Feller's loss. Sure, we still had a one-game lead, but we had to return to Boston for the next two, though we were hoping only one would be necessary.

It was, thanks to Bearden, again.

I could've started Gene in that sixth game, but chose to go with Lemon instead. That way I had Bearden in the bullpen, along with everybody else. And if a seventh game became necessary, he would pitch it.

The Braves, gambling that there would be a seventh game, held back their ace, Johnny Sain, and started Bill Voiselle.

We scored first on Dale Mitchell's double and my single in the third, but the Braves tied it in the fourth. Joe Gordon led off the sixth with a homer, and before the inning was over we got another run on a walk, single, and an attempted double play that wasn't made.

Lemon blanked the Braves again in the sixth and seventh, and we raised our lead to 4-1 on singles by Ken Keltner, Thurman Tucker, and Eddie Robinson. The Boston fans could see that the end was near for their heroes.

But not until our hero got to the mound again.

The Braves loaded the bases with one out in the eighth and I was faced with a major decision. Do I bring Bearden in and lose him for the seventh game if the Braves pull this one out? Or do I go with somebody else—Satchel Paige or Ed Klieman or Russ Christopher or maybe even Steve Gromek—and hope he can put out the fire?

Considering everything Bearden had done all year, my choice was easy.

Gene came in brimming with confidence and quickly retired Clint Conatser on a fly that scored one run. Then Phil Masi doubled for another run, cutting our lead to 4-3, which put me under the gun again. How much further do I stay with Bearden? Do I change pitchers now, or give him one more batter?

We talked and Gene convinced me he could get Mike McCormick, a veteran right-handed batter who'd hit .303 and had driven in the Braves' first run of the game. Two pitches later McCormick bounced back to Bearden and the threat was ended. Only one more inning, three more outs, and we would climax the greatest season anyone could ask for, including—especially— Bill Veeck.

Eddie Stanky was the Braves' first batter in the ninth and Bearden walked him. Connie Ryan went in to run and Sibby Sisti batted for Warren Spahn. Everybody, including the 40,103 fans in Braves Field, knew Sisti was going to bunt to get the potential tying run in scoring position.

He poked at Bearden's first pitch and missed it, let the second go for a ball, then popped up the third. For some reason that Ryan probably still can't explain, he broke for second and was doubled when Jim Hegan caught Sisti's popper and fired to first base.

That brought it down to one; just one more out and we would complete our amazing rags-to-riches season.

Tommy Holmes became that one more out. He flied to Bob Kennedy in left field and the world championship was ours.

Bearden had done it again.

But this time he wasn't carried off the field. Not that we weren't happy. It's just that we were too tired, too spent emotionally.

That's not to say we didn't celebrate. We did, on the train back to Cleveland.

In the course of the party Joe Gordon did it again. He called for quiet, raised his glass, and fixed his eyes on me across the club car.

"To the greatest leatherman I ever saw, to the damnedest clutch hitter that ever lived, to a doggone good manager, Lou," he said.

What a tribute!

And we all received an even greater tribute upon our arrival in Cleveland the next morning. A massive parade was held in our honor. We were cheered by hundreds of thousands of fans lining a five-mile route from Public Square, the center of the city, eastward to University Circle.

Never before and never since has there been such an outpouring of affection and praise for an Indians team as we received that Tuesday, October 12, 1948.

We received World Series shares of $6,772, then the most ever in baseball history. The Braves got $4,570 apiece, which also was a record payoff for the runner-up team.

But to me the greatest reward was not financial. It was the satisfaction of having proved my ability as a manager, as well as a player, and in providing the Cleveland fans with a championship that represented my gratitude for their support of me.

Goodbye, Bill

It was after we won it all in 1948 that Bill Veeck coined the expression: "Sometimes the best trades are those you don't make."

It was a reference, of course, to the trade he didn't make a year earlier that would have sent me to the St. Louis Browns for Vernon Stephens.

But he said it even better in another way that winter.

On January 25, 1949, Veeck tore up my contract that was to run through 1949 and gave me a new one through 1950 at a raise of $13,000, to $62,000 each year. This one included $25,000 to manage the Indians, the same as my previous contract, and $37,000 as a player, making me one of the highest-paid men in the game.

I know that doesn't sound like much, considering what major league players and managers are making now, but it was a lot of money then. Like all guys of my era, I often envy the salaries today's players are getting, but I also worry about what might be in store for baseball down the road.

What bothers me is that the big money and guaranteed, long-term contracts—especially *guaranteed contracts*—tend to destroy a player's dedication. When a fellow is making the kind of money players are getting today, and is assured of getting it for the next several years no matter what he or his team does now, where's the incentive to do better?

And when individual statistics are the main thing, it's only natural that the average guy is going to ask himself, "Why extend myself and take a chance of getting hurt? I'm going to be paid the same thing no matter what we do, whether we win or not."

I'm not saying everybody has that attitude, and I'm not blaming the players for accepting the money being thrown at them. It's the owners who created this monster.

But I'm afraid it's going to reach the point—if it hasn't already—where the average family can't afford to go to a game.

Million-dollar, guaranteed, long-term contracts were not a concern of anybody in 1949. There were a couple other things that hurt us that season and cost us a chance to repeat.

First, there was a natural letdown after the way we'd won the pennant and World Series in 1948. It was easy to believe we could do it again, do it even easier.

Even Veeck thought so, and said it often.

At the baseball writers' annual "Ribs and Roasts" awards banquet in January 1949, Veeck said in his speech: "Last year at this dinner I told you we had a chance to win the pennant. This year we have a better ball club and we should have an easier time."

I believe I was the most photographed athlete in the country that winter, and I must have attended more banquets and receptions and been asked to make more speeches than anybody. I don't believe I ate at home more than twice a week from the end of the World Series until spring training began—and I enjoyed every minute of the attention.

I'd had something to prove, remember? And I was still basking in the afterglow of our achievement.

Not only did the Indians win the pennant and World Series, I was named the American League's Most Valuable Player, Veeck the Executive of the Year, Gene Bearden the A.L. Rookie of the Year, and Bob Lemon the A.L. Pitcher of the Year.

Despite those honors, Veeck didn't stand pat.

We got pitcher Joe Haynes from the Chicago White Sox for catcher Joe Tipton, and then acquired another pitcher, Frank Papish, for pitchers Bob Kuzava and Ernie Groth in another deal with the White Sox. It wasn't that Veeck wanted Haynes or Papish so badly, it's just that he wanted pitcher Early Wynn and first baseman Mickey Vernon from Washington. And the only way Clark Griffith, owner of the Senators, would deal with Veeck was if he got Haynes in return.

Haynes, you see, was Griffith's son-in-law—and didn't I tell you Veeck was shrewd?

He also gave Griffith first baseman Eddie Robinson and reliever Ed Klieman for Vernon and Wynn, a deal that would pay dividends for the Indians down the road, though not immediately. Wynn had some arm trouble early in the season and won only eleven and lost seven, while Vernon hit .294 for us and Robinson .294 for Washington.

Steve O'Neill, who had managed the Indians from mid-1935 until he was dismissed in 1937, and was my manager at Buffalo in 1938, rejoined us as a coach after being fired by Detroit. Steve and I were good friends and I wanted to show my appreciation for all he'd done for me, even to the extent of helping me take the job of his son-in-law, Skeeter Webb, who'd been the Indians shortstop before me.

O'Neill replaced Muddy Ruel, who was moved up to assistant farm director under Hank Greenberg. Bill McKechnie and Mel Harder remained on the staff.

We also had some good-looking rookies coming to spring training: pitcher Mike Garcia, outfielder Minnie Minoso, third baseman Al Rosen, second baseman Bobby Avila and shortstop Ray Boone, though only Garcia and Boone would make significant contributions.

We really would have been in trouble without Garcia, who won 14 games and lost five, because Feller as well as Wynn started the season with a sore arm.

Boone originally was a catcher when he signed in 1942, but after spending three years in the service and the 1946 season behind the plate in the minor leagues, he was switched to shortstop. I know a lot of people said I resented him moving in on me, but it was my recommendation that he change positions because of his good hands and rangy build.

The fact that we had a great young catcher in Jim Hegan also figured in the decision.

But Boone couldn't handle shortstop on an everyday basis which, in retrospect, probably was my fault. I tried to get him to play the position the way I did, but we were two different types. He just didn't move well enough.

Boone played 76 games at shortstop that season and hit .252. He was traded to Detroit in 1953 and had four great seasons as the

Tigers' third baseman—which shows you how smart I was. After he was established at Detroit, Boone was quoted as saying, "Third base compared to shortstop is like stealing." We didn't consider moving him to third because we still had Ken Keltner, and Rosen was just coming up.

I hit .284 in 134 games, 88 at shortstop, 38 at third base, six at first base, and even one at second base, which should give you an idea as to how unsettled we were most of the season. Joe Gordon slumped to .251 and Keltner also was sidelined for a while with an injury and hit only .232 in 80 games, all of which was a far cry from what we'd done the previous season.

In 1948 our infield—Keltner, Gordon, Eddie Robinson, and I—hit a combined 97 homers and drove in 432 runs, which might have been a major league record. But in 1949 the infield, now with Mickey Vernon replacing Robinson at first base, and including Boone's production, had only 54 homers and 283 RBI.

With all that I've said so far, I shouldn't have to tell you that 1949 was quite a comedown for the Cleveland Indians and their player-manager.

We were 6-3 in April and 11-15 in May, at one point losing 10 out of 13 games. We landed in seventh place on May 23, and remained there for three weeks.

Then Frank Lane added insult to injury.

After we were shut out in both games of a doubleheader in Chicago in late May, Lane, the White Sox general manager, sent the Comiskey Park home plate to Veeck with a note that said, "We thought you might like to know what this looks like."

By the end of May, the date was May 31, to be exact, one of our loyal fans, named Charlie Lupica, built a platform atop a 60-foot flagpole in front of his drugstore on the east side of Cleveland and climbed it, vowing to stay there until we regained first place.

He remained there until September 23, after we'd been mathematically eliminated from the pennant race. Veeck, loving every minute of the stunt, had the pole—with Lupica still atop it—transported to the stadium, where Charlie made his descent.

That also was the night Veeck held "funeral services" for the 1948 pennant. He buried it behind the fence in center field and nearly 35,000 "mourners" showed up.

After we'd fallen into seventh place in May, it was a struggle for us the rest of the way. We managed to regain second and hold it for five weeks in July and August, but never spent a day at the top, much to the chagrin of Lupica, whose wife had a baby while he was sitting atop the flagpole waiting for us to get back into first place. The closest we got was two and a half games behind the Yankees in August.

We were all disappointed, nobody more so than I, unless it was Veeck.

New York won the pennant and Boston wound up second, again one game behind. We won our last seven games to beat Detroit out of third place, but it was small consolation as we finished eight games off the Yankees' pace.

Our record was 89-65, also eight games worse than the year before, and—probably even more significant, especially to Veeck—our attendance was off by nearly 400,000, falling to 2,233,771.

By mid-season, when it became evident that we were having problems, we didn't see as much of Veeck as before. He became aloof, distant. He was the type who always had to be on top.

Because we'd won the pennant in 1948, I managed the American League All-Star team, and was glad to do so—though it was small consolation for our lack of success trying to get back to the World Series. We beat the National League, 11-7, and Larry Doby became the first black player to appear in an All-Star Game for the American League. Joe Gordon and Dale Mitchell also played and contributed big hits in our victory. Jim Hegan and Bob Lemon were on the team but didn't get into the game.

Naturally, the rumors began early on that my days as manager of the Indians were numbered, never mind that my two-year contract ran through the following season. Veeck made several road trips with us but kept his distance and never had much to say to me directly, other than to wish us good luck.

I know that Veeck felt I was too much of a "hunch" manager, that I relied on my instincts instead of managing by the book. I'm sure that Greenberg thought the same. In fact, I think Greenberg, with his constant second-guessing of my decisions, had a lot to do with formulating Veeck's opinion of my managerial ability, and I resented it.

I confess, Greenberg was not one of my favorite people. I could take his second-guessing, but what I didn't appreciate was that he seldom gave me a reason for disagreeing with the things

I did. He was not straightforward, and our relationship—which was cool at best in the beginning—worsened as time went by.

My answer to Greenberg's and Veeck's belief that I was too much of a "hunch manager" was that my moves and decisions were made because I felt I knew my players and what they could do better than anybody else.

That's why I started Gene Bearden and installed Allie Clark at first base in the 1948 playoff, and did any number of other things that some would consider "unorthodox." When I went against the book it was because I felt I knew my players and what they were capable of doing.

As I've already said, injuries to key players hurt our chances in 1949. Feller's arm was sore for the first five weeks and he went 15-14, though Lemon (22-10) and Garcia (14-9) made up some of the slack.

But injuries weren't the whole story of our demise.

Gene Bearden, our hero of 1948, did a complete flip-flop, winning only eight games and losing eight. He lost control of his knuckleball, which had been his "out" pitch. Don't ask me why. Maybe he was throwing it too hard, or maybe too soft. Who knows? Gene himself couldn't provide an answer.

Some advice attributed to Casey Stengel, who'd been Bearden's manager at Oakland in 1946 and was the manager of the Yankees in 1949, might have been a factor in Gene's inability to win consistently as he'd done the year before.

According to reports making the rounds, Stengel told his players—and they told others around the league—that to beat Bearden they should lay off his knuckleball until he got two strikes on them, and make him throw his fastball or curve, both of which were only average at best.

And because Bearden had trouble throwing his knuckleball for strikes, he had to come in with fastballs and curves, and got hit. Hard. His earned run average in 1948 was 2.43; it soared to 5.10 in 1949.

Bearden was traded to Washington in 1950, and then to Detroit, St. Louis, and the Chicago White Sox. The poor guy never had another winning season. The most games he won were seven in 1952, and by 1954 he was back in the Pacific Coast League, where he pitched four more years without earning another ticket to the big leagues.

Satchel Paige flopped, too, losing the fountain of youth he'd apparently found in 1948. Satch won only four games and lost seven, and wasn't the easiest guy to handle. I didn't dislike Paige, but he marched to his own drummer and lived by his own rules. As long as he was pitching effectively, his idiosyncrasies could be tolerated. But he wasn't winning in 1949 and was released at the end of the season.

We wanted to bring Luke Easter up from San Diego, where he was murdering Pacific Coast League pitching, and was being built up to be the "black Babe Ruth." But the big first baseman had a knee injury that required surgery in July. When Luke was able to join us on August 11, he still had not completely recovered from the operation and didn't do us—or himself—any good.

The fact is, promoting Easter when we did, actually hurt him. So much was expected of the big guy, and when he didn't deliver—he failed to hit even one home run in the 21 games he played for us after being called up to Cleveland—the fans booed him unmercifully. I felt almost as bad for Luke as I'm sure he did.

Don't misunderstand. I didn't blame the Cleveland fans. I blamed the system and the situation that made it necessary for us to promote Easter at a time when his physical condition was less than 100 percent. Not only did the team need a spark, Veeck also was looking for something that would spark new interest in the fans.

Larry Doby, who'd established himself as a bona fide major league hitter and outfielder in 1948, also came in for criticism by the media and fans. He committed a costly base-running blunder in late July and was never allowed to forget it the rest of the season.

We were losing to the Yankees, 7-3, in the eighth inning and loaded the bases with nobody out. Doby, who was on third, tried to steal home against Joe Page on a 2-and-0 pitch. He was easily retired and the Yankees went on to win in front of more than 75,000 fans in the stadium, who booed Doby off the field.

Larry's only explanation was that he thought he could make it.

I had to reprimand him, though I did so with some misgiving. As I explained to the writers after the game, I didn't want to curtail Doby's aggressiveness because he basically was a good base runner. He just made a dumb mistake and those things happen in the heat of a pennant race when you're trying hard to win, but things are not going well.

Two months later, when we were on the brink of mathematical elimination from the pennant race, Doby got even with the Yankees—sort of—by stealing two bases, including home, in the first inning. But it didn't really matter as we went on to lose that game, too.

I'm sorry to admit that the frustration of losing also got to me, and I made a dumb mistake after we blew both games of a doubleheader in St. Louis in late August.

Those two losses to the Browns dropped us five games out of first place and I was really upset as I left the field. When a photographer tried to take my picture, I waved him off and stalked away. To the best of my recollection, I'd never done anything like that before or since. It wasn't the photographer's fault that we'd lost, or that we were struggling. It's just that I was so frustrated and let my French temper get the better of me.

At the beginning of this chapter I said there were a couple of things that hurt us in 1949 and pointed out that, first, we all suffered a letdown after the success we'd enjoyed in 1948.

Something else that was a major factor in our downfall began when Veeck was approached by Republic Pictures—or vice versa—about making a movie featuring the Indians. Everybody considered us a "hot" item and, to be honest, I was flattered and thought it was a neat idea, too.

I soon changed my mind.

The movie was called "The Kid From Cleveland" and starred Rusty Tamblyn, then a teen-aged actor, Lynn Bari, and George Brent.

The story featured Tamblyn as a juvenile delinquent who became a good boy because he wanted to be a big league ball player, a shortstop like his hero Lou Boudreau. I was very flattered. Brent was a sportswriter, Lynn Bari was his girlfriend, and all our players were to be involved, especially Johnny Berardino.

The advance publicity for the movie called it "the story of a kid, a city and thirty godfathers." The godfathers, of course, were our players. Even Veeck, Hank Greenberg, and trainer Lefty Weisman were in it. Berardino, an aspiring actor who has been a star of several television soap operas since his retirement from baseball in 1953, was a gangster in the movie. I played myself.

The filming began early in the season at League Park, and usually about nine o'clock in the morning. We'd break for lunch, then shower and dress in street clothes and a couple of hours later report to the stadium for our game that night. It was like being on the road every day and went on like that until about the first of June.

It was more than tiring; it also was a great distraction. I know it hurt me and there's no doubt it had a negative effect on the whole team. Though Veeck never admitted it, I've got to believe he was sorry he let us go ahead with it, but by then it was too late to back out.

The movie opened on September 2, ironically at a time we'd fallen well off the pace and were in a battle with Detroit for third place, instead of with New York and Boston for first.

Bill McKechnie and I went to the premiere with our wives and I'll never forget his reaction to one of the early scenes. The camera zeroed in on the first baseman—an actor, not one of our players—and when he threw the ball across the diamond McKechnie howled, "Oh, no! He throws like a girl," which he did. It was awful to anybody who knew anything about baseball.

It was not a very good movie, which is putting it mildly, in my opinion, and none of our guys made any money out of it, though we were supposed to if it did well.

It's still shown occasionally on television, but—thankfully—only late at night when few people are up watching, and those who are, don't care what they see.

Veeck had little to say when the season ended. He was having some personal problems and had left town. I went home to Harvey thinking what a difference a year had made.

Twelve months earlier we were the toast of baseball and I was besieged with invitations to make appearances all over the country.

But now, I tried to forget the frustration and disappointment of not being able to win the pennant, and to think about what we could do to get back to the top in 1950.

That also was the time that speculation began—denied at first by Veeck—that he had lost interest in owning the Indians and would soon be selling out.

The hottest rumor was that controlling interest in the franchise would be bought by one of Veeck's partners, Bob Goldstein.

Even Hank Greenberg, in his autobiography published in 1989, said it was his understanding that Goldstein would take over the club.

But on November 20, seven weeks after the season ended, the Indians were sold to a group headed by Ellis Ryan, a Cleveland insurance executive. The reported price was $2.2 million, nearly $1 million more than Veeck and his partners paid for the franchise a little more than three years earlier.

Ryan immediately announced that Greenberg, who had been vice president and farm director, would take over as general manager of the club.

As for me, Ryan was quoted as saying, "I understand Boudreau has another year to go on his contract." Period.

I wasn't sure how Greenberg felt, though I'd soon find out.

Goodbye, Lou

The 1950 season in Cleveland saw a changing of the guard in more ways than one after Ellis Ryan took over the team and put Hank Greenberg in charge.

And Greenberg wasted no time making over the Indians.

Ken Keltner was released and Al Rosen installed at third base.

Luke Easter, now fully recovered from his knee surgery, opened the season in right field but soon was handed first base, and Mickey Vernon would be traded back to Washington (in a deal that would be one of Greenberg's worst).

Bobby Avila, also up from the minors, would lean on Joe Gordon and soon take over at second base.

And Ray Boone was moving in at shortstop.

I hated to see Keltner go. We'd been together since 1939, when I first came up with the Indians, and were good friends. He was a real professional, one of the best third basemen I've ever seen and, in my opinion, one who also belongs in the Hall of Fame.

But Greenberg was right that Rosen was ready. I'm sure that Keltner knew it, too, and took the release like the pro that he was.

And when the time came for Gordon to go at the end of the season, he also handled it with class. Joe also was a dear friend of mine. His legs went on him, and when they did, he went downhill fast.

It's always sad when a player reaches the end of the road, but it happens to everybody sooner or later.

My coaching staff also was changed. My good friend Bill McKechnie—"Pops," as I called him, though he was "Deacon Bill" to others—was then 63 years old and decided to retire, though it proved to be only temporary.

Steve O'Neill, who'd rejoined me in 1949, also retired, though it also was only temporary. O'Neill, 58 years old, would return as manager of the Boston Red Sox three months into the season, replacing Joe McCarthy.

Another good friend, Oscar Melillo, returned. He'd coached for me when I first became manager of the Indians in 1942 and remained on my staff until he went into scouting. Muddy Ruel also came back to the field after a year as assistant farm director. Mel Harder remained and Al Simmons was hired to replace O'Neill.

So what was my status?

Greenberg was hard to read. As I've already said, he was not a favorite of mine, though I always had great respect for him as a player.

From the time he joined Veeck in the winter of 1947-48, and especially during the 1948 season, when I would meet with the two of them the morning after games, I felt that Hank did not have any great regard for my managerial ability.

I also knew that Greenberg was a great admirer of Al Lopez, who'd played for me in 1947, after a long career with Pittsburgh. Lopez retired after that 1947 season and Veeck—along with Greenberg, I'm sure—helped him get a job as manager of the Indianapolis Indians of the Class AAA American Association, then a Pirates farm club.

Indianapolis under Lopez won 100 games and the American Association pennant in 1948, and finished second with a 93-61 record in 1949. There was no doubt he was the Cleveland Indians manager-in-waiting—waiting for me to fail.

But I always was motivated by challenges, and 1950 certainly represented one.

I felt pretty good about what we had, especially our pitching staff that now featured Bob Lemon, and included Bob Feller, who also was facing a major challenge, to prove he was still one of the best in the game. Early Wynn, the pitcher we got from Washington in 1949, had overcome his arm problems, and Mike Garcia, the guy we called "Big Bear" who'd done so well as a rookie the year before, would be our fourth starter.

Our outfield again had Larry Doby, now an established star in center, flanked by Dale Mitchell and, initially, Easter, though Bob Kennedy soon took over in right field.

Easter was not a good outfielder—the guy was simply too big to move around out there—and his arm wasn't the best, either. But I wanted Luke's big bat in the lineup, along with Vernon's.

Jim Hegan had become one of the best receivers in baseball, which more than offset his low batting average (which wouldn't be so low by today's standards).

All things considered, I felt pretty good. I knew New York and Boston would be tough again, but I was confident we could compete, though I made no pennant predictions. Neither did Greenberg, a more conservative type than Veeck, though the same could be said of almost anybody.

We started the season slowly but climbed into third place by mid-June as Rosen and Easter were two of the hottest hitters in the American League.

Easter, the target of the fans' abuse in 1949 when he came up from San Diego and tried to play on only one leg, went on a hitting rampage during one stretch from early June until the All-Star break in mid-July.

Vernon, on the other hand, hit only .189 in our first 28 games and was replaced at first base by Easter, which also improved our defense as Kennedy, who took over in right field, was a good fielder and had one of the strongest throwing arms in baseball.

The installation of Easter at first base and the benching of Vernon led to one of Greenberg's worst deals. On June 14, one day before the trading deadline, Vernon was returned to Washington in exchange for Dick Weik, a reliever who pitched for us only briefly and not very well.

Vernon went on to play nine more years, even winning the American League batting championship with a .337 average in 1953. Weik appeared in 11 games for us in 1950, going 1-3 in relief, was back in the minors in 1951 and 1952, was traded to Detroit in 1953, and retired in 1954 with a career record of 6-22.

Easter, a genuinely nice guy, hit a monster home run on June 24, in a game against Washington, that I'm told has never been equaled in Cleveland. With a 6-1 lead in the sixth inning, I gave Luke the green light on a 3-and-0 pitch from Joe Haynes.

Easter swung, the ball jumped off his bat and I didn't think it would ever come down. It flew into the upper deck of the right-field stands at the stadium and I'm not sure I ever saw a ball hit harder. It was later measured at 477 feet and was Luke's second homer of the night and eleventh of the season. Easter went on to hit 28 homers that season, though Rosen would lead the league with 37.

There were two other memorable games at the stadium that season: the first on July 2, when Feller beat Detroit for his 200th major league victory; and August 2, when Doby blasted three consecutive homers in an 11-0 victory over Washington.

In his fourth and fifth trips to the plate, Doby walked and struck out as Lemon pitched his ninth straight victory for a 17-4 record.

We stayed in third place until the end of August, never climbing any higher or slipping any lower, until we got into September. Then, with the Yankees back in first place and the Tigers second, Boston overtook us and we fell into fourth.

While it's true we didn't win the pennant, I thought 1950 was a pretty good season. We won 92 games, three more than in 1949, and we did it with a young team that would be a contender for the next several years.

I was pleased with the rebuilding job we'd done. Avila batted .299 in 80 games after replacing Gordon at second base; Rosen, Easter, and Doby combined to hit 90 homers and drive in 325 runs; Lemon was the major league's winningest pitcher with a 23-11 record; Wynn won 18 games and Feller 16.

As for me, I knew my playing career was nearing an end, but I was confident I could still be a productive hitter and shortstop and had every intention of continuing as a player-manager, which compels me to set the record straight on something that was written in Greenberg's book.

I was supposed to have spoken to him about being a bench manager in 1951, which bothered him, he said, but it simply wasn't true. I planned to continue to play. I'd hit .269 in 81 games and driven in 29 runs. Boone, the heir to my shortstop job, hit .301 and drove in 58 runs.

But he also made 26 errors in the field (I made four), and I wasn't sure Boone was ready to take over at shortstop.

Everything considered—though our attendance dropped another 500,000 admissions to 1,727,464—I thought 1950 was a pretty good season for the Cleveland Indians and looked forward to staying with this up-and-coming young team.

Before I left Cleveland and went home to Harvey, Greenberg spoke to me about 1951. He indicated he wanted to re-sign me to the same contract I had for 1949 and 1950 that paid me $62,000. I told him I'd think it over, and that's the way we left it.

The media also thought I'd be back, as Gordon Cobbledick, the highly respected sports editor of the *Plain Dealer* wrote on November 7:

> "Ellis Ryan and Hank Greenberg studiously avoided saying anything about Lou Boudreau's position as manager or ex-manager, as the case may be, of the Cleveland Indians.
>
> "But in the process of ducking the questions tossed at them by a house packed with representatives of the press and radio, they made the answer so clear that when the official announcement of Boudreau's reappointment is released it will come as an anticlimax.
>
> Someone asked Greenberg if he would go ahead and complete a deal without consulting the Indians' 1951 manager, whoever he may be.
>
> "'Oh, no,' Hank replied. 'I'm only doing some preliminary work. I certainly won't complete any trades until I've talked them over with Lou.'
>
> "If that wasn't notice that Boudreau will be doing business at the old stand again next spring, it was sufficiently like it to serve until formal notice is forthcoming."

That *formal notice* came three days later, but wasn't what everyone expected, nor what I wanted.

But first, Ellis Ryan—not Greenberg—called and told me they were going to make a change. He said that out of respect for me and all I'd done for the Indians, they wouldn't try to trade me, they'd just release me, though two teams, Boston and Washington, had shown an interest in me.

This way, Ryan said, I could sign with a team of my choice, as a player, player-manager, or just a manager. He said my release would be in the mail, wished me luck, and hung up. That was that.

I was surprised and disappointed. I had always wanted to end my career in Cleveland as a bench manager, and thought I would.

I didn't hear from Greenberg, which also disappointed me, though in retrospect I should not have been surprised that he didn't call, that he left it to Ryan to inform me of the club's decision to let me go.

The formal announcement that I would be replaced came on November 10 in the form of a press conference called by Greenberg.

"Gentlemen," the newspapers reported that he said to the media, "here's your next manager of the Indians," and Al Lopez walked through the door from the men's room.

Greenberg was quoted as saying, "We knew we had a man as manager who was probably the most popular player in the history of the Cleveland Baseball Club. We also knew we had a fine, outstanding gentleman whom everybody loved.

"For one month we have been working diligently to get Lou a manager's job somewhere else. Today we learned of one club that was interested and I think he will have a job in the major leagues."

When the reporters called, I told them, "Naturally, I was quite shocked. I'm terribly sorry to leave Cleveland, for the fans were wonderful to me.

"As for Greenberg and Ryan, I have nothing to say against them. They're running the club. But it would have been better if they had made the change a few weeks ago and had given my coaches more time to find other jobs."

There was some reaction by the fans on my behalf, but apparently there never could be enough to change Greenberg's mind, as they had influenced Veeck three years earlier.

And with that my 12-year career in Cleveland came to an end.

The Hottest Seat

When Ellis Ryan let me go in Cleveland, he told me that Clark Griffith, owner of the Washington Senators, and Tom Yawkey, who owned the Boston Red Sox, were interested in me, which was true. But only as a player, a utility infielder at that.

Bucky Harris (who had been baseball's first "Boy Manager" in 1924 when he was 27 years old), was the Senators' manager, and his shortstops were Pete Runnels and Sam Dente, with Eddie Yost at third base.

My old friend Steve O'Neill had returned as manager of the Red Sox, and he had Johnny Pesky at shortstop and Vernon Stephens, a former shortstop, at third. I would have been a utility infielder there, too, if I chose to sign with Boston.

I had no problem accepting a part-time role. As I've said, I knew I was nearing the end of my playing career, but I was confident I could still be productive and wanted the opportunity to contribute as much as I could.

I also wanted—really *expected*—to manage again down the road, though I was not thinking along those lines at that time.

In fact, I withdrew from consideration for a managerial job in the National League.

A few weeks after the Indians fired me, I received a call from Branch Rickey, then general manager of the Pittsburgh Pirates. Mr. Rickey said they might replace Billy Meyer, who'd managed the Pirates in 1950 when they finished last in the National League with a 57-96 record, 33 1/2 games behind Philadelphia.

Mr. Rickey asked if I'd be interested. I said yes, but I wanted to know more about the Pirates' situation and what he had in mind. A couple of weeks later he came to Chicago to meet with me. There had been speculation in the papers that I was headed for the Pirates, but his visit was kept quiet.

I met him at Midway Airport with a fraternity brother of mine, Frank Frochauer, who was then a coach at my old high school, Thornton Township. Frank went into the airport to get Mr. Rickey while I waited in the car, out of sight, to avoid publicity.

We went to my home in Harvey and ate some of Della's apple pie and talked for an hour or so about the National League, the Pirates, my career with the Indians—everything but money.

Mr. Rickey said he was interested in me as a manager, but not a *player-manager*. I told him that would be okay if we reached the point where he wanted to commit to me and I wanted to commit to the Pirates.

I probably would have been willing to be a bench manager for him, but not for Hank Greenberg. At that point I would not have given Greenberg the time of day.

Still, I harbored some second thoughts about ending my playing career. I was the first to admit I had slowed up. But not that much, and I was in good shape. My ankles were bad, but no worse than they'd ever been.

Mr. Rickey left and said he'd get back to me, but before he did, Joe Cronin, the general manager of the Red Sox, and O'Neill got in touch. Cronin convinced me they really wanted me as a player.

Maybe it's just that I was flattered to still be wanted as a player, or that O'Neill, my old mentor, wanted me back with him.

It also was a matter of playing in Boston. I loved to hit in Fenway Park, and I knew the fans had never forgotten what Gene Bearden and Ken Keltner and Joe Gordon and I had done against the Red Sox in that exciting playoff game of 1948.

I accepted Cronin's offer of $45,000—which was $5,000 less than Washington was willing to pay me—and signed as a utility infielder with the Red Sox.

Contrary to some reports, there was neither a commitment made, nor even one implied that I would be considered to manage the Red Sox if the job opened. The way Cronin handled it, and something which I was more than willing to accept, was

simply that we'd let the future take care of itself. What would be would be.

The only commitment was on my part, to do whatever I could to help O'Neill and the Red Sox. In the 33 years since 1918 the only pennant they'd won was in 1946. Not only had they lost to Cleveland in the 1948 playoff, they also were beaten out by New York for the 1949 pennant on the last day of the season.

I called Mr. Rickey and told him I'd decided to sign with Boston. I respected him as a person and a baseball man, but the truth be told, I didn't especially want to go to the National League or to Pittsburgh, and I didn't particularly like the Pirates' personnel.

O'Neill and Cronin made me feel wanted right away. So did the fans. I was right. They remembered me and seemed glad to have me on their side. I'd always enjoyed playing in Fenway Park, and I liked wearing a Red Sox uniform.

I'd always worn No. 5, even in college, and am proud that my number was one of only three retired by the University of Illinois. The other two were Red Grange's 77 and Dick Butkus's 50, which puts me in pretty good company. My No. 5 also was retired in Cleveland, along with Bob Feller's 19, Earl Averill's 3, and Mel Harder's 18.

Vernon Stephens was wearing No. 5 when I got to Boston in 1951, so Cronin asked me if I'd wear his No. 4, which has since been retired by the Red Sox. I was honored to do so, and continued to wear it the entire time I was in Boston.

Cronin, incidentally, is another who'd been nicknamed "Boy Manager" in 1933, when he was hired at the age of 26 by his father-in-law, Clark Griffith, then owner of the Washington Senators.

Mr. Yawkey and I became good friends, too. Because I was accustomed to going to the park early on the day of a game, I ran into Mr. Yawkey quite often. He'd come down to the clubhouse, put on workout clothes and we'd go out to the field, throw a ball around, and play pepper. He was a fine gentleman and I'm sorry we couldn't do better for him.

It was a step down for me to return to the player ranks in Boston, but it really was no problem. I didn't pal around with my players when I managed in Cleveland, and with the exception of Ted Williams, I didn't pal around with many of my teammates on the Red Sox. It wasn't that I felt uncomfortable doing so, it's just that I was new on the team and kept pretty much to myself.

I used to go out to dinner a couple of times a week with Williams when we were home. He loved to sit around and talk baseball, fishing, and swimming, in that order, and we used to laugh about how upset he got when I used the "Boudreau Shift" against him.

Ted also was a very competitive guy, which I learned early on—and which cost me some money the first year I was in Boston.

When he'd pass me on the way to the plate, he'd often say to me, "Two-to-one for twenty bucks I get a hit." Sometimes Williams even laid odds he'd hit a home run, and he usually won then, too. The guy was amazing.

Ted Williams was, without a doubt, the greatest hitter I ever played with or against. Probably the greatest to ever play the game.

We finished third in 1951, but it wasn't a strong third. Our record was 87-67 and we wound up 11 games behind the Yankees.

We also were six games behind Hank Greenberg's and Al Lopez's Indians, though in a way I still felt they were *my* team because all the regular position players, as well as the starting pitchers, came up under me.

I played in 82 games, including 52 at shortstop, 15 at third base and two at first base. My batting average was .267 with five homers, and I drove in 47 runs, which I felt proved I could still play the game.

But when I got my last hit in late September of 1951, little did I realize there would not be another one.

When I reported for spring training in Sarasota, Florida, in 1952, I assumed my role would be the same, that I would share shortstop with Johnny Pesky and also spell Vernon Stephens at third base. Those two had switched positions in 1950 and 1951; Pesky played third in 1950, but went to shortstop in 1951; and Stephens, who'd been the shortstop in 1950, was moved to third in 1951.

Spring training barely got started when Steve O'Neill suffered a severe recurrence of the gout, which had bothered him off and on for several years. It became difficult for him to get around and he decided to retire.

Cronin offered the manager's job to Earle Combs, then a Red Sox coach. But Combs, a former star outfielder and teammate of Babe Ruth with the Yankees, declined. He felt he was too old and was satisfied being a coach, perhaps because the Red Sox always had a reputation for being a difficult team to manage—and Boston always has had the reputation for being a difficult city in which to manage.

While Cleveland used to be known as the "Graveyard of Managers," managing the Red Sox in those days was called the "hottest seat in baseball." A big reason was that there were nine daily papers in Boston and the surrounding area, and a flock of baseball writers on each one. The reporters were constantly looking for a "scoop"—and constantly worried about being scooped, which made it difficult for everybody.

One columnist was particularly tough, especially on Ted Williams. For some reason Dave Egan, better known as "Colonel" Egan, hated Williams and always found an excuse to rip him.

When Combs said no to Cronin, Joe offered me a two-year contract at the same salary, $45,000, I was making as a player, to take over as manager. I didn't give him a chance to change his mind and accepted immediately. It was another challenge and I couldn't wait to get started.

Combs stayed on as a coach and I brought "Pops" back, Bill McKechnie, and another old friend, Oscar Melillo. They joined George Susce and Paul Schreiber, who'd also been on O'Neill's staff.

I thought we had a pretty good team and would be a contender if our pitching came through, which always seems to be the case with the Red Sox. Our ace was Mel Parnell, who won 18 games in 1951.

We started well enough, going 10-2 the first month of the season.

But then, on April 30, we lost Williams. The Korean War was on, and Williams, a fighter pilot in the Marine reserves, was called to active duty. It was a shame, for both the Red Sox and Williams, as he'd previously lost three seasons, 1943-45, to World War II, and wouldn't return to baseball until August of 1953.

We had nobody to pick up the slack—but then, who could ever replace a Ted Williams?

We fell into fifth place by the All-Star break, climbed to third and held it from late July into mid-September, but collapsed at the end. Our won-lost record the final month was 7-20.

Stephens slumped from .300, 17 homers, and 78 RBIs, to .254, seven homers and 44 RBIs. Pesky's average fell off drastically, too, from the .313 he'd hit in 1951, and before the season was a month old, Cronin pulled off one of the biggest trades in baseball history.

In retrospect, it was a good deal for the Red Sox, though we didn't come close to being a contender, finishing worse than the year before, in sixth place, 19 games behind New York, with a 76-78 record.

On June 3 we traded Pesky, first baseman Walt Dropo, pitcher Bill Wight, infielder Fred Hatfield, and outfielder Don Lenhardt to Detroit for third baseman George Kell, shortstop John Lipon, outfielder Hoot Evers, and pitcher Dizzy Trout.

I've read where Hal Newhouser, then a Detroit pitcher, called the deal "the worst of all-time," for the Tigers; of course, that might be a slight exaggeration.

Kell, Lipon, and Evers moved into the starting lineup for us, and Stephens became our utility infielder, replacing me—which is ironic considering how badly Bill Veeck wanted to replace me with Stephens four years earlier in Cleveland, before the fans convinced him to back down.

My playing career ended in early May of 1952 after just two official at-bats—without a hit. I knew I was finished when I got hit by a pitch from Virgil Trucks in a game against the Tigers. I didn't see the ball until the last instant and threw my left hand up to protect my face. It broke a bone in my hand, and even if I had wanted to play, I couldn't continue.

By then I realized it was time to hang up my spikes, though it was a difficult decision. But rather than try to hang on and perhaps be booed, I didn't put myself back on the active roster after my broken hand healed.

I can't remember my last hit, which came in September of 1951, or who I got it against because, frankly, I didn't think it would be the last one. I fully expected to play a full season in 1952.

It was disheartening to have to quit, but again, it happens to everybody sooner or later.

Something else that happened in 1952, and also was very disheartening, concerned Jim Piersall, then one of the Red Sox' brightest prospects. Jim was a center fielder, a quick, agile youngster with great athletic ability, good hands, and a strong arm.

Early in the season I realized we had a gaping hole at shortstop that neither Pesky nor Stephens nor I could plug. I also tried a rookie, Milt Bolling, but he couldn't cut it either, and I was at the end of my rope.

Before we made the trade to acquire Lipon, I decided to experiment with Piersall and give him a shot at shortstop. I still believe he could have been a great one.

But the pressure of making the switch apparently was too much for Jim to handle. He played 30 games at shortstop and, at times, showed flashes of brilliance.

But he also began to act strangely, and his antics on the field became disruptive and distracting. However, we still felt we had a chance to contend for the pennant—if we had a capable short-stop—so we made the deal with Detroit.

And because Piersall's behavior continued to be inconsistent, we decided to send him to Birmingham of the Class AA Southern League, hoping the demotion would straighten him out.

It didn't, and in retrospect, I realized we should have ar-ranged to get Piersall professional help long before we finally did. He was no different during his brief stay at Birmingham; in fact, his antics there got him ejected from four games, the final time on July 17, resulting in a three-day suspension.

We brought Jim back to Boston on July 19 for an extensive medical examination that led to his hospitalization. He did not play the rest of the season, but came back to us in 1953 and played 151 games—all of them in the outfield—and hit .272.

At the end of the 1952 season Mr. Yawkey told Cronin to rebuild the Red Sox with younger players. He held a meeting with the scouts and told them he was committing $800,000—a lot of money then—to find and sign the best college and high school players the money could buy. The amateur draft wasn't in effect then, and teams could sign anybody they wanted.

The decision also was made to bring up the best kids in the farm system and let them play in 1953—and the best were outfielder Tommy Umphlett, catcher Sammy White, and in-fielder Ted Lepcio.

The infusion of young players transformed the Red Sox from a veteran team that scored a lot of runs, but had not won a pennant in six years and no longer was a contender, into an exciting, up-and-coming young team that *would* be good, but also was not a contender then.

One of my first decisions was to replace Dominic DiMaggio with Umphlett in center field. My decision was based on the fact that I'd seen too many fly balls that should have been caught, fall for hits in left-center and right-center field in 1952. DiMaggio, then 36 years old, had lost a step and I wanted a younger, faster center fielder.

Naturally, Dominic didn't like it, and I understood how he felt.

But he had to understand how I felt. As manager, it was my job that was on the line.

Though our record improved in 1953 to 84-69, we were less of a contender than we'd been the previous season. Only during a two-week period in late July did we climb as high as third place, but finished fourth, this time 16 games behind the Yankees.

Cronin renewed my contract for 1954 at the same $45,000 salary I'd been making, but this one was for only one year, and the message was clear. I had to produce.

Williams returned from Korea to play the final 37 games in 1953, but by then it was too late to help bail us out, and his presence in the lineup in 1954 wasn't enough to keep us from backsliding further.

We continued to shuffle players, including trading Kell to the Chicago White Sox, always trying to bolster our pitching staff, but without much success.

Kell and I had become very close friends and it was very difficult—probably the most difficult thing I ever had to do as a manager—to tell George he'd been traded.

Even sadder was what happened to the rookie first baseman who broke in with us in 1954, a former Marine and Boston College football star named Harry Agganis. He was nicknamed the "Golden Greek," and hit .251 with 11 homers and 57 runs batted in. Less than a year later Agganis would die of pneumonia.

As for me, I could sense the end of my managerial career with the Red Sox was approaching. We spent most of the first half of the season in last place, and climbed to fourth with a 69-85 record at the end, a whopping 42 games behind none other than my former team, the Indians, who won a major league record 111 games.

We finished strong, but it wasn't good enough, not in Boston, where the manager's seat is the hottest in baseball.

I don't think anybody could have done better with the teams I had. I inherited a group of aging veterans and spent the next two years rebuilding the Red Sox. It was not easy.

And so, a couple of weeks after the season ended and before I went home for the winter, Cronin called me into his office.

I was disappointed, but not surprised, to hear him say, "Lou, I'm sorry, but we've got to make a change."

From Bad
To Worse

When Joe Cronin let me go about two weeks after the 1954 season ended, he told me, "I've got a spot for you to manage. It will be Kansas City if you want it, but we can't say anything about it now. Think it over and let me know."

At the time Kansas City didn't even have a major league team, but Cronin knew it would be getting one soon.

I told him I didn't need to think it over, that I wanted the job, and thanked him—although, in retrospect, I probably shouldn't have. I went from a bad team in Boston to one that would be even worse.

But at the time I felt pretty good about it because the fans in Kansas City desperately wanted a major league team, and were so happy to get one, they didn't care how bad it was. I expected to be given time to build the club into a winner, that within three to five years we'd begin to see daylight.

Cronin had inside information that Connie Mack was negotiating to sell the Philadelphia Athletics. Mack had owned the A's from the time the American League was founded in 1901, and also had been their field manager for 50 years, until he stepped down in favor of Jimmy Dykes in 1951.

But Mr. Mack was then in his 90s and his family had no interest in keeping the franchise. The National League Phillies had become Philadelphia's favorite team, and the A's season attendance declined from 600,000-plus in 1952, to less than 400,000 in 1953, and all the way down to about 300,000 in 1954.

The buyer of the Athletics would be Arnold Johnson, who operated a profitable vending machine business in Chicago. I didn't know him, but he knew of me going back to my basketball and baseball playing days at the University of Illinois, and that I'd managed the Cleveland Indians when they won the pennant in 1948.

Cronin said Johnson would contact me once he closed the deal with Mack, and the American League gave him permission to transfer the team to Kansas City. Until then there'd been only two franchise moves in baseball, the Boston Braves to Milwaukee in 1953 and the St. Louis Browns to Baltimore in 1954.

The deal was finalized and approved by the other 15 major league owners in mid-December and, just as Cronin had said, Johnson called. We had no problem working out my contract. It was for two years at $25,000 per year, and I was excited to be back in the game.

It didn't bother me that my salary was quite a bit less than what I'd made in Boston. I probably would have signed for anything Johnson offered. I really wanted the job and looked forward to facing a new challenge.

Johnson said he was committed to building a winner in Kansas City, and our master plan was for the Athletics to be a pennant contender in three to five years. There was no doubt in my mind that we could, though it would not be easy considering the team we inherited.

For the previous few years Mr. Mack had been unloading his higher-salaried players to meet expenses. As a result, the Athletics, who'd been one of baseball's all-time greatest teams in the late 1920s and early 1930s—and even challenged for the pennant that my Cleveland club won in 1948—had deteriorated into one of the worst of all time.

Which is why Johnson was able to make such a good deal to buy the A's.

According to newspaper reports, Johnson paid $3.6 million for the franchise and Connie Mack Stadium in Philadelphia. Then he turned around and sold the park to the Phillies for $1.6 million.

Next, after getting approval to move the franchise to Kansas City, Johnson sold the radio broadcast rights to A's games for the next five years to the Schlitz Brewing Company for $1 million, which brought his investment down to $1 million.

But Johnson still wasn't finished.

He took Blues Stadium, where the minor league team had played and which he'd owned for several years, and sold it for $250,000 to the city, which brought it up to major league standards and renamed it Municipal Stadium.

Then Johnson leased it back—at a very sweet deal, of course.

Did I say Arnold Johnson was a good businessman?

He hired a local man named Parke Carroll as general manager. Carroll was the former sports editor of the *Kansas City Journal Post,* and when the paper folded, he became general manager of the Blues.

Parke was a good fellow, but I was never too sure about his baseball expertise.

Johnson and I made several trips to Kansas City during the winter of 1954-55 to generate support, and the reception we got was sensational, from both the fans and media. There were only two newspapers in town, the *Star* and the *Times,* both owned by the same publishing company that had spearheaded the effort to get a major league franchise. One reporter, Joe McGuff, covered us for both papers, and it was a lot easier to deal with him than it was with the media in Boston.

Something else in our favor was that everybody was tired of the Kansas City Blues being a farm club of the New York Yankees in the American Association.

What they didn't realize, at least not then, was that the relationship between Kansas City and the Yankees would continue, with only a slight change.

During the next few years, we traded some of our best players to the Yankees, including Clete Boyer, Enos Slaughter, Art Ditmar, Bobby Shantz, Ryne Duren, and Harry Simpson. There was a real shuttle operating between Kansas City and New York—and too many of our good young players went, and we wound up with players the Yankees no longer wanted.

Carroll made the deals, though I must say I had some input in all of them except the one for Boyer, in which 12 players were involved, six from each team.

We sent Ditmar, Shantz, Jack McMahan, Wayne Belardi, Curt Roberts, and Boyer to New York, and got Billy Hunter, Rip Coleman, Mickey McDermott, Tom Morgan, Milt Graff, and Irv Noren. None of those we got did much for us, while Boyer, Ditmar, and Shantz were major additions to the Yankees.

I don't know if it was true, but there was a lot of speculation that Johnson owed a favor to his friend, Del Webb, one of the Yankees' owners, for helping him buy the Athletics from Connie Mack, and generate support among the other owners to give their approval to move the franchise.

The first thing I did in Kansas City was to hire Oscar Melillo and George Susce, who coached for me with the Red Sox. Harry Craft, who'd managed the minor league Kansas City Blues, and Burleigh Grimes, the old spitball pitcher who'd been a coach for the Athletics in Philadelphia, were my other two coaches. They replaced Bill McKechnie and Del Baker, who'd been on my staff in Boston, but retired after I was fired by the Red Sox.

Everybody's attitude was optimistic when we reported to West Palm Beach, Florida, for spring training but, realistically, I knew it was not a sound team. We had some good hitters in Vic Power, Hector Lopez, Slaughter, and Gus Zernial, but not much pitching—very little pitching, in fact. Ditmar would be our biggest winner, and his record was only 12-12.

But the fans loved us. I'll never forget our first game. Former President Truman threw out the first ball, and Connie Mack was among the crowd of nearly 33,000 that saw us beat Detroit, 6-2. You would have thought we'd just clinched the pennant.

We didn't win a whole lot after that, and except for Opening Day, we never climbed higher than fifth place. But we drew almost 1.4 million fans and, much to the surprise of everyone, we finished sixth, though our record was an awful 63-91 and we were 33 games behind the Yankees.

Because of the kind of players we had, I felt compelled to do a lot of shuffling to get the best out of each of them, and earned— unfairly, I believe—a reputation for being a "platoon manager."

I know a lot of players resented my strategy and thought that I overmanaged sometimes. But what I did was play the percentages. I felt I knew my personnel better than anyone else and what I tried to do was match up my hitters against the other team's pitchers according to strengths and weaknesses. It wasn't simply a matter of left vs. right and vice versa.

Gus Zernial, our best power hitter, was one who didn't hide his belief that he should play every day, against all pitching, and it bothered him when he didn't.

Gus pointed out that he hit 30 home runs in 120 games and 413 at-bats in 1955, which averaged out to one homer every 13.7 trips to the plate.

That same season Mickey Mantle led the American League with 37 homers in 517 at-bats, or one every 13.9 trips to the plate.

Zernial's argument was that—at least theoretically—he could have hit as many homers as Mantle if I had let him play every day. My rebuttal was that Zernial did as well as he did because of the way I matched him against some pitchers and kept him away from certain others.

I did the same with guys like Elmer Valo and Enos Slaughter, who also were getting up in years, and got the best out of them, too.

Vic Power was a special problem. He was one of our good young players and might have been the slickest-fielding first baseman in the league. He also was one of the most popular guys on the team. He'd played for the Kansas City Blues in 1953, and hit .319 for us in 1955. The fans also liked Vic because he was such a showman—or a "hot dog," as the players called him.

The only problems I had with Power concerned his behavior off the field. But on the field he was a fine player, a good hitter— he batted .309 and .319 our first two seasons in Kansas City, though his average slipped to .259 in 1957—and was a magician with his defensive ability.

I'd talk to Vic, but he was an adult, and there wasn't much we could do except trade him, which I wouldn't do. (After I left Kansas City, Parke Carroll dealt Power to Cleveland for Roger Maris, and Maris then was traded to the Yankees and broke Babe Ruth's single-season home run record with 61 in 1961.)

Another player I remember well was a relief pitcher named Tommy Lasorda—the same Tommy Lasorda who would become manager of the Los Angeles Dodgers 20 years later.

Tommy's record in 1956, his only season with us, was 0-4 in 18 games, which tells you how good he was.

He was always experimenting in the bullpen, and one day before a game he told me he'd developed a knuckleball that he was eager to use in a game. "It's working real good and I can throw it for strikes," he said.

I said I'd give him a chance the first time we needed relief, which we did later that night. When I put Tommy in the game I told him not to use the knuckleball until he got two strikes on a batter—which he did, the first guy he faced.

Lasorda threw his knuckleball and it landed about 30 feet up on the screen behind home plate, and two runners came in to score.

I told him I never wanted to see his knuckleball again.

But that wasn't all that was bad in 1956. Instead of making progress as I expected, we regressed and fell into last place, finishing with a 52-102 record. It was very discouraging.

We started the season well enough, but collapsed in mid-May and stayed in the basement except for two brief occasions when we climbed into seventh place.

The fans still loved us, but fewer of them paid to see us play—400,000 fewer, in fact—which always grabs the attention of an owner, including our Arnold Johnson.

Art Ditmar was still our best pitcher, again winning 12 games, but instead of a .500 record as he had in 1955, he lost 22 games in 1956, and nobody else won in double figures.

Vic Power had another good season but was the only regular to hit over .300, and Zernial slumped to .224 with 16 homers.

Our last-place finish didn't help my status, though I was re-signed for 1957 at the same $25,000 salary I had been paid, and the fall-off in attendance had a drastic effect on our well-laid master plan to rebuild the A's.

Because of fear that even more fans would quit on us if we continued to lose in 1957 while developing young players for the future, Parke Carroll went out and picked up three veteran pitchers to "stabilize" our staff, which was the way he put it.

They were Ned Garver and Virgil Trucks from Detroit and Tom Morgan from the Yankees. All three were near the end of the line and would combine to win only 24 games in 1957.

We also acquired Ralph Terry, then a 21-year-old rookie, from the Yankees, and he went 4-11.

Terry was the kind of young pitcher the Athletics should have developed and stuck with. But two years later, after he became a winning pitcher, Terry was traded back to the Yankees with Hector Lopez, a pretty good infielder, for three players who did little for the A's, which also illustrates what I had to say earlier about the shuttle between Kansas City and the Yankees.

On Sunday, August 4, we lost to the Orioles in Baltimore, 5-

0, dropping our record to 36-67. After the game we went to Chicago for a three-game series against the White Sox.

I went home to Harvey to spend some time with Della and the kids, and when I reported to Comiskey Park for the game the next night, Parke Carroll was waiting for me in my office.

I knew why he was there.

"Lou, I've talked with Mr. Johnson and we think it's best to make a change," he said. "I hope you understand."

I didn't, and I told him nobody could have done better with the players we had. We'd scrapped our building program and wound up with as bad a team as we'd inherited from Philadelphia.

But that didn't change anything and I was out of a job. I wasn't resentful because, the truth be told, the travel and the losing—*especially the losing*—were getting to me. In a way, I was relieved that it was over.

Strange as it may sound, what bothered me more than anything was being fired in my own backyard.

Fame Is Fleeting

After Parke Carroll fired me, I wasted no time cleaning out my office. I wanted to leave the clubhouse before the players arrived on the team bus. It was easier that way.

But Harry Craft, one of my coaches and a good friend, was there early and stopped me on the way out. He said Carroll asked him to take over the team the rest of the season, but he wouldn't do it without my assurance that it was okay.

I appreciated Harry's concern and knew he'd been loyal, that he hadn't undermined me. I told him to take the job with my best wishes.

After I got home to Harvey, I received a phone call from Jack Brickhouse, the television announcer for station WGN in Chicago, who did broadcasts of Cubs and White Sox games. Brickhouse also was in management at WGN, which had just contracted for the radio rights to do the Cubs games in 1958.

At first I was reluctant to talk to Jack, or anybody in the media, because I didn't want to come across as being bitter or critical of Arnold Johnson or Parke Carroll or anybody in baseball.

I kept in mind what Bill McKechnie, good old "Pops," had told me a long time earlier: "When you're being interviewed you have to remember that the fellow with the microphone or typewriter always has the last word."

But Brickhouse wanted to interview me for a job, not a story. "You are a great interviewee, and with your knowledge of baseball and background in the game, you should consider getting on this side of the microphone, doing the interviewing," he said.

It was very flattering coming from someone with the stature of Jack Brickhouse, one of the all-time great sportscasters, who would win the 1983 Ford Frick Award presented by the Hall of Fame "for major contributions to the game of baseball."

I'd done some radio work in college after the Big Ten ruled me ineligible in 1938, but I never thought about a career in broadcasting because I always planned to play professional baseball.

But then, since being fired by the Athletics—and having grown weary as I was of all the travel and being away from my family so much—Brickhouse's suggestion suddenly sounded interesting.

He offered to arrange an audition and I accepted, though I still had some misgivings. Until then there'd been only a few ex-jocks in broadcasting, which shows how far ahead of everybody Brickhouse was in 1957. Now every professional announcer has an ex-jock for a partner.

Brickhouse and Jack Rosenberg, then sports editor of WGN, simulated a baseball broadcast. Rosenberg, now manager of sports for the Chicago Tribune Radio Network which includes WGN, created a series of different game situations, and Brickhouse asked me to comment on them as though we were actually broadcasting a game.

He'd set me up with something like, "Lou, the Cubs have runners on first and third with two out, what can we expect?" Or, "Lou, what do you think the manager will do now that the score is tied and so-and-so is coming to bat with two out and first base open?"

Brickhouse said he was convinced that I could add a new dimension to a baseball broadcast by just letting my thoughts come out, by saying what I anticipated would happen, or by giving my reaction to what did happen, and by explaining things that listeners might not understand, like why a manager did this or that in certain situations.

This went on for a couple of hours and I guess I did pretty well, which surprised me. I also was surprised that I actually enjoyed it, despite my nervousness. I kept worrying about making a grammatical mistake, or worse, that some clubhouse language might slip out of my mouth.

Brickhouse and Rosenberg told me to relax, to just be myself and say whatever came to mind as though I were sitting in the stands explaining the intricacies of the game to somebody who liked baseball but didn't know it from an insider's viewpoint.

They apparently liked what they heard and offered me a contract to do Cubs games when they moved to WGN in the spring of 1958. I would work with Jack Quinlan, a young broadcaster who had been covering the Cubs on another Chicago station.

The money was not as much as I'd been making as a manager, but I was satisfied. My family never wanted for anything, and didn't after I went into broadcasting.

The most important thing to me was that I'd continue to be involved in the game I loved. I'd still be close to my friends in baseball, the managers, coaches, and players, even the guys pounding typewriters in the press box. I found most of the reporters—but not all of them—to be honest, accurate, and fair, though I didn't always agree with them or appreciate the things they wrote about my players or me.

That winter, instead of studying scouting reports and statistics and evaluating possible trades as I'd done so often in the past, I practiced my diction, enunciation, and delivery, things like that, getting ready for my career in broadcasting that would continue for 30 years.

I also got to know my family better because the pressure of trying to rebuild losing ball clubs or figuring how to stay on top no longer dominated my thinking during the off-season.

Barbara, our oldest child, had grown up and was getting ready for college. In two years she would marry Paul Golaszewski, a former University of Illinois quarterback. They have four children and are living in Frankfort, Illinois.

Sharon, then going on 15, had already met her husband-to-be, Denny McLain, though it would be six years before they'd get married.

My oldest son is Louis. He's not Lou junior because his middle name is Harry, after Della's father. Lou was 10 when I went into broadcasting. Eight years later he'd join the U.S. Marine Corps and be sent to Vietnam, where he was wounded three times during his six-month tour of duty.

We in sports often talk about the courage it takes to stand 60 feet from a pitcher throwing a baseball 90 or 95 miles an hour, sometimes even faster, or to go over the middle to catch a football, or to take a chance of being undercut while leaping to shoot a basketball through a hoop, or to get checked into the boards by a hockey player skating 35 miles an hour, or to block a puck traveling 80 miles an hour.

But it takes real courage to put your life on the line as Lou did, who lives in Phoenix with his wife Vicky and six children.

Our second son, Jim—James Douglas—was born in 1959, a year after I started at WGN. He's named after Dr. J. D. Logsdon, my first baseball coach when he was superintendent at Whittier grade school in Thornton Township. Dr. Logsdon was like a second father to me after my dad passed away in 1939.

Jim was a pretty good left-handed pitcher and was drafted by the Cubs after he played for Arizona State in the College World Series in 1982. He pitched two years in the Cubs farm system and two more with the Baltimore organization but never got higher than Double-A.

Jim had good control for a left-hander and an effective sinker. But then somebody tried to teach him a screwball, he hurt his arm, and his baseball career was ended. He and his wife Rita live in Oak Lawn, Illinois.

I'm often asked about my son-in-law Denny McLain, and understandably so. What Denny did in 1968 when he won 31 games for Detroit and lost only six has to be the greatest season-long performance by a pitcher since Dizzy Dean went 30-7 in 1934—perhaps the greatest since Lefty Grove was 31-4 in 1931.

Denny got into trouble with the law in 1984 and served two years in a federal penitentiary. It hurt Della and me because we knew it hurt Sharon and their four children. While he was in prison we helped Sharon and the kids as much as we could, physically, emotionally, and financially.

The way I handled it with Denny was that I let him know I was available, that if he wanted me for anything, advice or help of any kind, he could come to me, which he never did.

In his autobiography, *Strikeout*, Denny admitted he'd been stupid. I agreed, and that was that. The first time he came home from prison and we all got together, it was like nothing had ever happened, which was the way it should have been.

We all go through life having to learn lessons of one sort or another. Denny's was tougher than most of us face, and he had to learn the hard way.

But the important thing is that he learned—and he's a better person for it.

Sharon and Denny also have suffered the tragic loss of their oldest daughter, Kristin, who was only 26 and had just been married when she was killed in an automobile accident near Detroit on March 20, 1992. You never get over something like that; you only survive it.

Della and I are proud that Sharon stuck by Denny throughout his trouble, and that they're doing well now. Since 1990 he's had a three-hour, politically-oriented talk show five days a week on a Detroit radio station, and it's amazing how well-informed he is on so many subjects. He also is co-host of a half-hour sports show on television every Sunday.

I wish I could claim some credit for Denny's success as a pitcher, but I can't. He did it all himself. I was always too busy with my own career.

Denny had the same makeup as Early Wynn. He was one of those tough pitchers who went right after the batters with his best stuff and dared them to hit it.

I only saw him pitch in the big leagues twice, but he was very good both times.

I was there when he beat St. Louis, 13-1, in the sixth game of the 1968 World Series. Denny had lost the first and fourth games, but kept the Tigers' hopes alive in the sixth game, and they won the series the next day.

I also covered one of Denny's games in Atlanta in 1972, his last season. He came on in relief for the Braves and pitched very well for three innings. I wanted him to do well, of course. But I confess, I also was pulling for the Cubs to win after he left the game. They didn't and Denny was credited with the victory.

While I never had a chance to offer Denny any baseball advice, I can take credit for introducing him to Sharon in 1956. He was the star of a championship Babe Ruth team in Markham, Illinois, not far from Harvey.

I was in Chicago with the Athletics and was asked to present a trophy to McLain and his teammates. I took Sharon with me. She met Denny and remembered him when he signed a professional contract with the White Sox a couple of years later. She wrote Denny a letter of congratulations, he replied, and they began to date when he came home at the end of the season.

They were married in October 1963, and when he got up with the Tigers the next year, he usually was identified as "Lou Boudreau's son-in-law."

But in 1968, after Denny pitched the Tigers to the American League pennant and world championship, suddenly I became known as "Denny McLain's father-in-law."

Such is fame.

Another Fork
In The Road

I was pleased that WGN wanted me for the Cubs broadcasts and flattered, of course, that two real professionals like Jack Brickhouse and Jack Rosenberg had recommended me despite my lack of experience.

Both assured me all I had to do was be myself, that I shouldn't worry about making grammatical mistakes. They reminded me I would be on the radio because I knew baseball, not because I was an expert on the English language.

I also felt fortunate to be at home with the team my father and I had followed from the time I was in grade school. I'll always consider myself a Cleveland Indian, and always be grateful to the Cleveland fans for their loyalty to me. But the Cubs were my team from the time I could pick up a ball and throw it, and I was happy to be with them.

At the same time, I was disappointed to be taking off my uniform after 20 years in professional baseball, almost 19 of them in the big leagues. I had mixed emotions. A part of me wanted to be back in the dugout, calling the shots, though another part of me was satisfied to be starting a new career.

Della handled it as she had from the beginning of our life together, when I shocked everybody by applying for the job of managing the Cleveland Indians. As she told me in 1941, and repeated whenever we reached a fork in the road, whatever I wanted, she wanted, too.

And so I became a broadcaster, and would be one, with only a brief interruption, for 30 years, covering Big Ten football and

Chicago Bulls basketball, in addition to the Cubs on WGN, and doing interviews after Chicago Blackhawks hockey games.

In the beginning it was difficult for me to refrain from being critical. It wasn't that I was inclined to second-guess. I'd been second-guessed enough in my 15 years as a major league manager to know how unfair it is to have somebody on your back all the time saying—after the fact—that you should have done something else.

I was more concerned about a tendency I might have to be critical of a bonehead play. I was always a stickler for doing things the right way, for players to execute the fundamentals properly, and to anticipate the correct reaction in a given situation.

To put it bluntly, I was intolerant of stupidity on the field by professionals. I didn't like dumb players when I was managing, and I knew I wouldn't like dumb players when I was broadcasting.

And with the Cubs in those days you didn't have to be an expert to find fault with them. They'd been a second-division team for 11 consecutive seasons, including four last-place finishes, and wound up tied with Pittsburgh for seventh place in 1957.

Their leader was Ernie Banks, "Mr. Cub," a wonderful player and a wonderful person. Their winningest pitcher that season was Dick Drott, a rookie whose record was 15-11, but who'd win the grand total of only 12 games in the next six years before coming to the realization that he should get into another line of work.

Banks hit 43 homers and drove in 102 runs, and except for him and a few others, I can tell you without fear of contradiction that it was not easy to refrain from criticizing the Cubs.

But despite their problems and losing record, Jack Quinlan and I clicked from the beginning. He was young and enthusiastic and eager to do well after moving over to WGN from a smaller Chicago station. He previously worked in Peoria, Illinois, and was a protege of both Jack Brickhouse and Jack Rosenberg.

Neither of us upstaged the other. Jack reported the action and I tried to anticipate what would happen, though I consciously guarded against being a manager myself.

When I was in uniform I always said I knew my players' strengths and weaknesses better than anybody else. And that's the way I operated from the booth, with the assumption that nobody knew a player's capabilities better than his manager.

The only criticism I had of players was if their attitude was bad, which, unfortunately, is the case with many present-day professional athletes in all sports. In my opinion they're given too much, too soon, before they earn it, and too many of them believe they're bigger than the game they play.

But the fact is, it's the owners' own fault. They created this monster themselves.

The Cubs had a great offensive team in 1958 and were a little better than they'd been. But not a whole lot.

Ernie Banks hit .313 and led the National League with 47 homers and 129 runs batted in, and three others acquired in trades—Dale Long, Lee Walls, and Bobby Thomson—also came through big. They combined with Banks for a total of 112 homers and 358 RBI. Alvin Dark also was obtained to play third base, and hit a solid .295.

But the Cubs still had no pitching. Their leading winner was Glenn Hobbie, and his record was only 10-6. They were lucky to tie St. Louis for fifth place.

Banks had another sensational season in 1959, hitting .304 and again leading the league with 45 homers and 143 RBI, but there was virtually no improvement in the Cubs' record or their standing. They again tied for fifth, this time with Cincinnati, and as usually happens, the manager, Bob Scheffing, was fired.

Scheffing's successor was Charlie Grimm, who'd led a charmed life with the Cubs since he joined them in 1925. "Jolly Cholly," as he liked to be called, was a close friend of Cubs owner Philip K. Wrigley.

A hard-hitting first baseman in his playing days, Grimm was named manager of the Cubs for the final 55 games in 1932, when they won the pennant. They won it again in 1935, but Grimm was fired in 1938 with 28 games left in the season.

But that didn't finish Charlie with the Cubs.

Wrigley rehired him in 1944 for a second term, and a year later the Cubs won another pennant. However, after just 50 games in 1949, Charlie was dismissed again. He took over the Boston Braves in 1952 and remained as their manager when the franchise moved to Milwaukee in 1953.

When Grimm was fired by the Braves after just 46 games in 1956, Wrigley came to the rescue again. He made Charlie a vice president, which positioned him for a third term as manager when Scheffing was fired at the end of 1959.

But that third term didn't last long. Only 17 games, 11 of which were losses, including seven on an eight-game road trip that ended on May 4 with the Cubs in last place.

When I got to Wrigley Field the next day, I was told that John Holland, another Cub vice president, wanted to see me.

My first reaction was that I'd said something wrong on the air and was going to catch hell. Instead, Holland asked me to take over the team. He told me Grimm resigned—his exact words were, "Charlie said he was reading a magazine at three in the morning with the lights off. His nerves were shot and he couldn't take anymore of the way the team was playing."

The plan was for me to trade places with Grimm. I would take over as manager of the Cubs, and Grimm would replace me in the broadcast booth.

Before I gave Holland an answer I called Ward Quaal, president of WGN. I wanted to be sure it was okay with the station for me to return to the dugout, and he said the door would be open whenever I wanted to come back.

Once again I had mixed emotions, except this was opposite from the way I felt three years earlier, when I exchanged my uniform for a microphone.

I wasn't a rookie broadcaster anymore, and Jack Quinlan and I were doing well. The station liked us and, more important, the listeners did, too. We were getting a lot of mail, most of it positive.

But I was only 43 and still—at least then—a baseball manager at heart.

Della knew, too, that this was another challenge I couldn't resist, although, hindsight being 20-20, I probably should have. The 1960 Cubs were not a sound club, and Grimm had done neither the team nor his successor any favors.

Before I accepted the job, which would pay me $20,000 for the remainder of the season, I told Holland that I wanted a contract beyond 1960. It would be important for the players to know I wasn't just a fill-in guy, an interim manager, because there was so much to be done to rebuild the Cubs.

You didn't need to be an expert to realize that Grimm had never placed much emphasis on the proper execution of fundamentals, which I knew had to be stressed in spring training for a team to be successful. All Grimm ever did was throw out some balls and tell them to play a game. He definitely was not a fundamentals guy.

Holland told me not to worry, that a contract beyond 1960 would be taken care of later. As it turned out, I should have settled it then and there.

One of the first moves I made was to recall Ron Santo. He'd been a catcher in the minors, but I moved him to third base. Don Zimmer, who was nearing the end of his playing career, had been playing that position and helped Santo make the switch—and in effect, helped Santo take Zim's job.

Santo did well, and old reliable Ernie Banks had another great season, but our overall offense fell off. We also were still short—*very short*—of pitching, and we never got it turned around.

There was an initial spurt when I took over and we climbed out of the basement and into sixth place. But it was only temporary, and we were able to beat out Philadelphia for seventh place by only one game. Our record was 60-94, 54-83 under me. We finished 35 games behind Pittsburgh. It was awful.

But I felt we were capable of great improvement in 1961, and I was already thinking about spring training when I went home in October. I took for granted I'd soon be hearing from Wrigley and Holland about a contract.

When I did, in late November, it wasn't what I expected, and didn't please me. Wrigley, who always prided himself on being an innovator, came up with a plan that sounded crazy—and subsequently proved to be just that.

A former Air Force colonel named Robert Whitlow apparently sold Wrigley on the idea of having a team of rotating coaches, instead of one single manager. It was based on the system that worked well in professional and big-time college football.

The Cubs' version would be called the "College of Coaches." It would include 10 coaches in all. Four of them would be designated "head" coaches, and each would serve for 10 days or two weeks at a time at running the team.

Wrigley liked it, he said in the papers, because, "I went to the dictionary and looked up the word 'manager.' The definition I found was 'dictator.'"

He also was quoted as saying he was "tired of firing managers." This way he'd have, in effect, four managers at the same time, and whenever he got tired of one, or the Cubs weren't playing well, he could rotate one of the others into the top spot.

The contract I would be offered for 1961 was to be one of the head coaches. I quickly declined. I couldn't believe the Cubs were serious, but Holland said Wrigley definitely planned to give it a try "for at least a year, maybe two."

Personally, I don't believe Holland liked the plan any more than I did, though he would never disagree with Wrigley.

My argument was that revolving coaches would create all kinds of discipline problems because each would have different rules, and some would be more strict than others.

They'd also have different styles of managing, and different theories on strategy, which also would create confusion and disorder.

I told Holland that I didn't think it would work and I couldn't go along with it.

Then I called Ward Quaal and asked if WGN's door was still open to me. It was, and once again I was back in broadcasting—and this time I hung up my uniform for good.

Time To Go

The "College of Coaches" became a reality in 1961, thankfully without me. I proved to be right—it didn't work, and didn't last long.

The Cubs again finished seventh the first year of the change, and hit rock-bottom in 1962, losing 103 games, until then the most in franchise history.

Equally important to those involved was that the new system introduced by Cubs owner Philip K. Wrigley became the butt of jokes throughout baseball.

They were teased everywhere they went. Fans would yell to the head coach, "When are you going to call a classroom meeting and paddle your boys?" and "What's going to happen next week when you're not here?"

The reporters got into it, too. Everybody made fun of the Cubs, not because of the way they were playing—though they weren't playing well—but because of the College of Coaches.

I still remember the lead of a story by Ed Prell in the *Chicago Tribune* when Vedie Himsl, the first of the head coaches, started his two-week stint. It went like this: "Vedie Himsl was hired as the Cubs manager today, and at the same time was given two weeks notice."

It also created, as I had expected, confusion and disorder among the players. They never knew who was in charge, whose rules to obey.

In fairness to Wrigley, I should say that he wanted to win so badly he'd take almost anybody's advice, which I learned early in the season that I managed the Cubs.

The Cubs and White Sox played an exhibition game every year for the benefit of kids' baseball in Chicago. It had rained the morning we were to play in 1960 and the field was wet and sloppy. I used a minor leaguer in place of one of our regulars to be sure he didn't get hurt.

We lost the game and it didn't mean anything to me, but it did to Wrigley. Afterwards he called on the phone and scolded me. "I want you to know that I want to win all the time, not only the National League pennant, but I also want to beat the White Sox anytime we play them. Even in an exhibition game."

When Jack Quinlan and I were on the air during the time of the revolving head coaches, we handled the situation with kid gloves and studiously avoided any criticism of the system. We agreed that the less we even mentioned it, the better it would be for everybody, including the coaches themselves.

But that didn't change my personal opinion that it was a crazy idea, as I'd made clear to John Holland when I declined to be part of it.

The first group of head coaches consisted of Himsl, who'd been the Cubs farm director, Harry Craft, my former coach at Kansas City who succeeded me when I was fired by the Athletics, Lou Klein, and Elvin Tappe.

Craft, Klein, and Tappe had been coaches under Grimm in 1960, and were inherited by me when I took over the club.

The staff also included six coaches who'd travel through the Cubs' farm system. Each of them took his turn managing and instructing the minor league teams. In 1961, they were Bobby Adams, Dick Cole, Rip Collins, Goldie Holt, Fred Martin, and Verlon Walker.

That first year the Cubs won 10 and lost 21 under Himsl, then went 7-9 with Craft in charge, 5-7 when Klein took over, and were 42-53 for Tappe. Except for the first four weeks of the season, they occupied seventh place all the way.

Wrigley ordered a couple of changes in 1962, but they weren't enough to make a difference. Even the fans realized the system was flawed. Attendance fell to 609,802, lowest in the major leagues and the smallest total in Cubs history since 1943.

A drop like that at the box office always catches the attention of an owner, as it did Wrigley.

That was the year the National League expanded to 10 teams, and even one of the new franchises, Houston, finished ahead of the Cubs, which also registered on Wrigley.

To further add insult to injury, Houston's manager—*full time*—was Harry Craft, who had been hired away from Wrigley's "College of Coaches" the winter of 1961-62.

Himsl returned to his duties as farm director and was replaced by Charlie Metro, who joined Klein and Tappe as the staff of head coaches was reduced to three. Their records in 1962: Tappe, 4-16; Metro, 43-69; and Klein, 12-18.

The Cubs never got higher than eighth, marking the sixteenth consecutive season they finished in the second division. It tied a major league record for futility—a record that would be broken in 1963 and be extended for four more years.

Even more damning than the 193 losses charged against the College of Coaches those two seasons was a comment by Don Elston, then a reliever for the Cubs. Looking back at those two seasons, Elston was quoted in the *Chicago Tribune*:

"There was jealousy among the coaches. When one guy was the head coach, some but not all of the other coaches did nothing to help him. They sat there waiting for their turn. It was an unhappy time."

The baseball establishment also doubted the value of Wrigley's system of revolving coaches, though those who were quoted chose their words carefully so as not to offend Wrigley.

One story in the *Chicago Tribune* reported, "Then-Commissioner Ford Frick, when asked if he approved a manager-less Cubs, said, 'My only concern is that (Wrigley) has nine men on the field.'

"National League President Warren Giles was evasive. 'I'd rather not be quoted on that,' he said.

"American League President Joe Cronin, who wasn't beholden to Wrigley and didn't need his vote, was more blunt. 'I'd feel a lot better with one chief and more Indians,' said Cronin."

Finally, wisely, Wrigley got tired of the jokes and criticism and disbanded the College of Coaches. He hired as manager Bob Kennedy, who'd played right field for me in Cleveland when we won the pennant and World Series in 1948.

Kennedy was a good baseball man and in 1963 turned the Cubs' record around to 82-80. It was the first time they'd finished over .500 in 11 seasons, though they still wound up in seventh place. They slipped back to 76-86 in 1964, and when they lost 32 of their first 56 games in 1965, Kennedy was fired.

It was during spring training of that season that I lost my partner, Jack Quinlan, who'd become more than a colleague. He was a very dear friend.

But for the grace of God, I would have been with Jack when he was killed in an automobile accident in Arizona on March 19, 1965.

The Cubs trained in Mesa then, and Jack and I went to Chandler, about 20 miles away, to play golf because the Cubs were off that day. I'd promised my kids - we had all four of them by then—that I'd take them to an amusement park in Phoenix that afternoon, which was the reason Jack and I drove separately.

After our golf game I headed back to Mesa to pick up my family. Jack stayed in Chandler to play another round.

That night, after I'd taken the kids to the amusement park, Della and I went to the dog races. I was paged, and at first, we feared something had happened at home.

It was Jack Brickhouse. He was at the coroner's office and gave me the terrible news.

On his way back to Mesa earlier that night, Quinlan crashed into the rear of a parked trailer truck and was killed.

It was such a shame. Jack was only 38 and in the prime of his life and broadcasting career. He'd worked so hard to get where he was and just like that his life was snuffed out, his marvelous voice stilled forever. He left a wife and four children.

Brickhouse and I accompanied Quinlan's body home to Chicago. It was very sad. Something like that makes you realize how quickly things change.

Though Quinlan's death was a devastating loss, I was fortunate that Vince Lloyd, another real professional, was available to step in as play-by-play announcer and be my partner. Vince had been working with Brickhouse at WGN on television broadcasts. We also fitted together perfectly.

When the Cubs continued to struggle in 1965, Kennedy was replaced in late June by Lou Klein, who'd been retained as one of the coaches, but they still finished eighth.

The following winter Wrigley made another change. He hired Leo Durocher, who'd managed the Brooklyn Dodgers from 1939 through 1946, and part of 1948. Leo was forced to sit out the 1947 season because he was suspended by Commissioner Happy Chandler for "conduct detrimental to baseball."

He returned to the Dodgers in 1948, but didn't stay all season. Only 73 games, in fact, 35 of which the Dodgers won. Then Durocher was fired.

But he quickly surfaced again—and again was the center of a storm of publicity. When Leo was around, things were seldom peaceful.

A week after the Dodgers let him go, Durocher replaced Mel Ott as manager of the New York Giants, the team Brooklyn fans loved to hate. Leo continued at the helm of the Giants through 1955, when he was not rehired, and was out of baseball again until he served as third base coach for the Dodgers from 1961 to 1964, then Wrigley brought him back in 1966.

I knew Durocher from the time our teams—my Cleveland Indians and his Giants—had trained in Arizona and barnstormed north together in 1949 and 1950.

Overall, I liked Leo, though there were many times I *disliked* him. He would be warm and charming one minute, and obstinate and vindictive the next.

But I always respected him as an excellent manager. He knew the game, never missed anything on the field, and usually got the most out of his players.

Because he enjoyed the verbal give-and-take with reporters, Leo often put his foot in his mouth. Considering how long he'd managed in the big leagues I was surprised how many times he said things that were better left unsaid.

One of them was a statement he made at the press conference announcing his hiring as the Cubs manager in 1966. "I am sure of one thing," he declared with great solemnity. "This is not an eighth-place team," which the Cubs weren't.

They finished tenth that first season under Durocher.

In my job at WGN, I worked with Vince Lloyd on Big Ten "Game of the Week" broadcasts right from the start in 1958. Vince and I also did Bulls games in the National Basketball Association for several years in the 1970s.

I even got involved in broadcasts of Blackhawks games in the National Hockey League with Lloyd Pettit, which I'm sure surprised a lot of people.

Though I'd only played intramural football at the University of Illinois—except for those two days I practiced with the varsity at Coach Bob Zuppke's request—I knew the game, and analyzing it with Vince Lloyd on the radio was not difficult.

Basketball was even easier for me because I'd played so much in high school, college, and as a semi-pro before going into professional baseball with the Cleveland Indians.

Basketball has changed so much, probably because everybody wants more offense, though I liked the game better in my day. It's no longer a non-contact sport as basketball was designed to be. Nowadays a player practically puts his life on the line when he drives under the basket, and everybody runs with the ball, they're almost never called for a traveling violation, which is not the way the rules were written.

Something else I don't understand is how everybody—even many high school kids—can dunk the ball. I couldn't and I don't remember many in my day who could. It must be that the balls are smaller and the athletes bigger—and better. The two-hand set shot also was big when I played, but not anymore. I don't see anybody shooting that way now.

But I guess the fans like it because basketball is more popular than it's ever been.

It was my experience in hockey that few knew about. I grew up with the Bobby Hulls and Gordie Howes and always liked the game. Believe it or not, I even played hockey two years for my college fraternity team, though I confess I needed plenty of help from others to do so.

Because my ankles were so weak (and troubled me throughout my baseball playing career), I couldn't ice skate worth a darn. But I was able to stand up on skates, and my reactions always were good, so my intramural coach asked me to play goalie, which I did—and pretty well, too.

I'd glide to the cage on the arms of a couple teammates at the beginning of a period, and they'd come back out and help me off the ice at the end.

So I knew something about hockey, though my job on Blackhawks broadcasts was to do pre- and postgame interviews, which I think I did well because I've always been the inquisitive type. The answer to one question usually leads to another question.

Those quick reactions that made me a pretty good hockey goalie in college also probably saved Durocher from being fired by Wrigley long before he was replaced by Whitey Lockman in 1972.

First I should tell you that one of Leo's favorite pastimes was to tease people. But only his friends. If he didn't like you, he wouldn't bother you. He was especially tough on me when we'd tape his six-minute pre-game show, "Durocher in the Dugout."

Sometimes I'd have to restart the interview four or five times because Leo would cut loose with an expletive that would have gotten both of us fired if it had gone out on the air. Or he'd make some uncomplimentary reference to one of our sponsors. It was like a game to him, trying to slip a profanity or a nasty remark past me.

Leo always enjoyed my frustration when I'd have to stop the recorder, rewind the tape, and start all over. There were times I'd really get angry, and whenever I did, Leo would slap me on the back and say, "C'mon, Lou. Lighten up. Can't you take a joke, old buddy?"

Once, in fact, I got so mad at Durocher that I refused to do the show anymore with him. Vince did it in my place, and then patched things up between us.

As I said, I liked Leo—though there also were times I didn't. He could be very demeaning. I'd been a successful manager myself and didn't deserve to be treated that way by Durocher.

It was in early August 1969 that I saved Leo's job. The Cubs were steaming along in first place, seemingly on the way to their first championship season since 1945, and everything looked good.

Vince Lloyd and I flew to Los Angeles to join the Cubs for their series against the Dodgers and met Milton Berle on the plane. We talked and I invited him to be our guest that night at Dodger Stadium. Berle asked if I'd introduce him to Durocher and some of the players and I told him to join me on the field about 45 minutes before the game. He was thrilled.

Leo and I taped the "Durocher in the Dugout" show before Berle arrived. But unbeknownst to me, something was wrong with my recorder and our engineer couldn't pipe the interview back to Chicago.

By then Berle had arrived and Vince Lloyd called from the booth to say we had to do the Durocher show over.

And because it was late, we had to do it live.

I got the bright idea to involve Berle in the interview, which was okay with Durocher. When I got the signal that we were on, I introduced Berle and told him to ask the first question—which was a mistake.

He said to Durocher, "It's great that the Cubs are doing so well, Leo, but they've been up there before and blew it. Do you think you can keep them in first place this time?"

Though the Cubs were leading the division by 10 or 11 games, Berle's question sounded more like a suggestion that they'd fold again in the stretch.

Durocher, always sensitive to criticism, even the implied variety, bristled, and started to tell Berle what he could do to himself.

The first word out of Leo's mouth was, "Go —," but that quickly, before he spoke the second word, I yanked the microphone away from his face and out of hearing range. As I said, I always had good reactions. And in this instance, Durocher was fortunate that I did.

Philip Wrigley was a very conservative and proper gentleman, and if the four-letter word that Durocher was about to speak had reached the airwaves, Leo probably would have been fired on the spot.

Because of my quick reaction, Berle's question as to whether the Cubs could hold on to first place went unanswered by Durocher.

And because it did, no sooner was the interview finished than Vince Lloyd got a call in the broadcast booth. It was from the engineer at WGN in Chicago, who said the phones at the station began to ring as soon as the Durocher show was over.

Fans wanted to know what Durocher had said about the Cubs' chances of winning the division.

It turned out they didn't. The Cubs were in first place by nine games on August 9, but blew it. The New York Mets, another expansion team, was fourth by 13 games with 54 to go, but went 40-12 in the final two months to win the division, beat Atlanta for the pennant, and defeat Baltimore in the World Series.

The Cubs, who won only 22 of their last 50 games, wound up second. It was their best finish in 24 years, but it was small consolation to Wrigley or any of us close to the team, or to the fans.

Durocher lasted only two and a half more seasons. He was fired in July 1972 with the Cubs' record 46-44, and once again he was back in the game almost immediately, which says something for his reputation as a manager. A month and a half later Leo replaced Harry Walker as manager at Houston, where he remained through the following season before he retired.

I missed my give-and-take with Leo—though I didn't miss the times he embarrassed me, whether it was in good fun or not.

One of those occasions took place in 1972 when we were in Montreal and had an open date. Some of us decided to go the local harness racetrack and, as I rode the elevator down to the lobby of the hotel, I ran into Glenn Beckert, the Cubs second baseman.

Beckert didn't want to go to the track, but asked me to bet his uniform number, 18, to win the daily double. I also was supposed to back it up, to bet 81, on the double, but we got to the track a little late, I was rushed, and just got a bet down on 1-8.

When the No. 8 horse won the first race, it occurred to me that I didn't back up Beckert's bet. I told one of the guys I was with, "I hate to say this, but I sure hope the No. 1 horse doesn't win the second race." He said, "Don't worry, it won't. The favorite is 3-to-5 to win. The No. 1 horse won't come in."

But it did and the daily double paid $1,200, third highest in the history of the track. I was sick. What would I tell Beckert?

I figured I'd better tell him before he heard the results on the radio or got an early paper and thought he won twelve hundred bucks. I talked my way into the general manager's office and tried to call Beckert at the hotel. He was out, but I told his roommate, Ron Santo, what had happened, that I didn't back up Beckert's bet and he didn't win, and told him to be sure to tell Beckert.

Santo did. But he also told a few others, and Durocher heard about it.

When I boarded the team bus the next day, Durocher really let me have it.

"Boudreau, you lying s.o.b.," Durocher greeted me. "I've heard about people screwing their friends like you did to Beckert last night. If you ever did something like that to me, I'd call WGN and have your wages garnisheed."

Did I say Leo liked to tease his friends? I'll tell you again that he did. Very much.

But basically, my relationship with Durocher was good, as it was with those who followed him as managers of the Cubs—Whitey Lockman, Jim Marshall, Herman Franks, Joey Amalfitano, Preston Gomez, Lee Elia, Charlie Fox, Jim Frey, Gene Michael, Frank Lucchesi and Don Zimmer—until my broadcasting career ended in 1988.

During that time I also was teamed up with great partners. Jack Quinlan and Vince Lloyd were followed by Milo Hamilton, Dewayne Staats, and Harry Caray.

I worked the longest with Vince. We were together for 20 years, until 1984 when he moved over to WGN-TV to do Cubs and White Sox games. During our time together we also had a call-in show on the radio when we weren't on the air with the Bulls. I always enjoyed the banter with the fans.

I never pretended to be the most eloquent analyst, and I'm the first to admit that I sometimes fractured English grammar. I still blush when I think of the mistake I made early in my broadcasting career.

It was after the last game of the season and we were signing off. I said something like, "I know a lot of you listeners probably are critical of my grammar and sentence structure, but I think I've improved over the course of the year. I plan to take some professional courses during the winter and I'll try to do even better next season."

And then I said, "In the meantime, I want to thank everybody who's *wrote* to me."

No sooner did the word come out of my mouth than I couldn't believe I'd said it.

There also were times during my early years on the radio when we had to read commercials live, instead of their being taped as they are now. We'd often get a commercial handed to us at the last minute and wouldn't even have a chance to look at it before we had to read it on the air. And when you have 10 or 12 of those a game, it can be really tough. There'd be times I'd be worrying more about reading the commercial than I did about what was happening in the game.

Vince Lloyd still kids me about one commercial I had trouble with—and which I'd still have trouble reading if I had to do it today.

It was for a savings and loan that was giving away flowers as premiums for new accounts. On this particular day the bank was offering a potted rhododendron. I stuttered and stammered but never got more than "Rhode" out of my mouth. I still have trouble pronouncing the name of that plant.

But as Jack Brickhouse and Jack Rosenberg, my first two mentors at WGN always told me, I was sitting behind a microphone, alongside professional broadcasters like Jack Quinlan and Vince Lloyd because of my background and experience in baseball, not radio.

It was my job to explain why something was happening on the field and, because it did, what might happen next, as I would if somebody sitting alongside me in the stands asked the question.

I tried to not talk down to those who didn't know a lot about baseball, and I tried to not talk up to those who did know the game.

I was disappointed when WGN told me in January 1988 that my contract would not be renewed. I was not given a reason. I guess the station just felt that 30 years were enough.

In retrospect, perhaps it was. The time to quit comes to everybody.

Summing Up

"There are hitters in the Hall of Fame with higher lifetime batting averages, but I do not believe there is in the Hall of Fame a baseball man who brought more use of intellect and advocation of mind to the game than Lou Boudreau."

Baseball Commissioner Bowie Kuhn introduced me with those words at my induction into the Hall of Fame on July 27, 1970.

It was the happiest day of my life. There can be no greater reward for a player.

As I responded then, "My prayers have been answered."

And the telegram I received from President Richard Nixon was icing on the cake:

"This is a worthy tribute not only to your outstanding performance in the game, but also to your fine record of community service and devotion to fair play. The writers really got their story straight this time."

I like to think the commissioner's statement was a reference not only to my performance as a player, but also to my ability as a manager, which I had to prove often.

It was once said that managing a major league baseball team is more difficult than being president of the United States.

I'm not sure that's completely accurate, but there is some truth to it. Especially since the arrival of television and the advent of arbitration and free agency in baseball, all of which have resulted in the escalation of salaries beyond the wildest dreams of those of us who played in my era.

When I took over as manager of the Cleveland Indians in 1942, and throughout most of my 16-year managerial career, I didn't have to worry about the demands on my time by television, as is the case today.

Actually the easiest part of managing in the big leagues is running the game for nine innings on the field, when your only thoughts are winning, and how to do it—not what to say in front of a camera before and after the game is played.

I can appreciate what television does to promote baseball and how it contributes to the popularity and prosperity of the game which, of course, is so important to the owners.

But it also has created a catch-22: it's the huge income that teams receive from television that is the major cause of baseball becoming such big business. And it's the emphasis on business and money that bothers me about baseball now. There is little loyalty on the part of most players to their teams and vice versa.

If I were managing in the big leagues today, I probably would be considered a heel by a lot of reporters in both the print and electronic media. I wouldn't allow my clubhouse to be open as much as it was.

My reasoning is simple. The clubhouse is the players' home away from home and when they're there, things often are said that shouldn't be reported. Guys also tend to pop off more now—*much more* now—than they used to, and a lot of times when it gets in the papers the player being quoted decides he won't talk to the press anymore, even though he's the one who made the mistake.

Another reason it was easier in my time to deal with players who were not as team-oriented as I liked was that a 50-dollar fine meant something then.

But now, because of those multimillion-dollar, long-term, guaranteed contracts, virtually every player (with the exception of rookies) makes more money and has greater security than his manager.

Now, too, there's a maximum of five hundred dollars that players can be fined—and, believe it or not, many of them carry that much money and more in the pockets of their jeans.

I've even heard of cases where players have offered to pay *in advance* for their next violation, and if that doesn't make it difficult for a manager, I don't know what does.

But despite their advantages—their *wealth*—I doubt that today's players have as much fun or enjoy the game as we did when most fellows needed a second job during the winter to make ends meet.

Now, with agents and business managers handling the financial affairs of players, baseball is more of a business than a game, and that's a shame.

Before a club can make a trade, it needs a lawyer to examine the contracts of the players involved, which is not the way it was supposed to be.

I'm glad I didn't have to worry about those things when I was in the game.

The hardest thing for me as a player was to get a hit off Tommy Bridges, who had the best curveball I ever saw, and Hal Newhouser, who never threw a baseball that went straight. They were the two toughest pitchers I ever faced, though I always considered myself fortunate that I never had to bat against Bob Feller and Bob Lemon.

If I were managing today and had a well-rested Feller and Lemon on my staff, I'd have trouble picking one over the other to start a game we absolutely had to win. They were the best in baseball in their prime, and among the best of all time.

I found that handling pitchers—the good, the mediocre, and the not-even-mediocre—was the most difficult part of my job as manager of the Indians, Boston Red Sox, Kansas City Athletics, and Chicago Cubs. When to change a pitcher, or stick with him in a jam, was the toughest decision, as it must be for every manager.

I was not a good handler of pitchers my first couple of years but soon came to the conclusion that it's better to replace a pitcher too soon than to leave him in a game too long. It was a theory recommended by "Pops," my old friend and coach Bill McKechnie, which I accepted and practiced the rest of my career, often to the displeasure of my starting pitchers.

But making a difficult decision and sticking with it is a big part of being successful, which is one of the reasons Leo Durocher was, in my opinion, the best manager in the game during my era, and also must be considered among the all-time greats.

If I owned a club, I would have hired him. I also would have liked to play for him and, if he'd been willing to step down, I would have added him to my coaching staff in a minute.

I've already said that Durocher was not the easiest guy to get along with. He had faults as a manager, as everybody does, and one of them was that he got on the umpires too much, though that sometimes was a ploy, part of his strategy. But his knowledge of the game was amazing. Even more important was that he knew his players so well, their strengths and weaknesses, which is necessary to deal with 25 diverse personalities and get the best out of each of them.

It's impossible to handle all players alike. Every individual is different and requires different treatment, though team rules must be applied and enforced uniformly.

Durocher managed in the big leagues for 24 years, had a winning record in all but four of those seasons, and won three pennants—with Brooklyn in 1941 and the Giants in 1951 and 1954. His teams won 2,010 games, sixth most of all time, and he's one of only seven managers to exceed 2,000 victories.

Leo was not a great player—his career batting average as a shortstop for four teams was only .247—but he played 14 full seasons in the big leagues, which says plenty about his ability.

Does he belong in the Hall of Fame? Absolutely, on the basis of his managerial record. In my opinion, Durocher is one of several old-timers who have been overlooked by the Veterans Committee.

Another is Mel Harder, a great pitcher who was one of my coaches in Cleveland and deserves credit for helping transform Bob Lemon from a light-hitting third baseman/outfielder into a Hall of Fame pitcher. So, too, should Joe Gordon, Phil Rizzuto, and Marty Marion, in my opinion.

Gordon, as great a second baseman, hitter and inspirational leader as ever played the game, is on my personal all-star team, along with Ted Williams, Joe DiMaggio, and Roberto Clemente in the outfield, with Hank Aaron moved to first base because he could play anywhere you put him, Brooks Robinson at third, Al Lopez, and Jim Hegan behind the plate, and Bob Feller and Hal Newhouser my right- and left-handed pitchers.

And if you have to ask who my shortstop would be, you'll find his name on the cover of this book, a guy who loved playing the game, who always played it as hard as he could, and who will be forever grateful for having had the opportunity to do so.

Epilogue

After more than half a century covering all the bases in baseball—on the field, in the dugout, and behind a microphone—I have but one regret, and it's not that I was born 40 or 50 years too soon, as many friends have suggested.

Sure, if I'd come along in 1978 or 1988, I'd have made much more money than my peak salary of $63,000 a season, which equates to about one-third of what David Cone and Greg Maddux are paid *per start*, or about $20,000 less than Barry Bonds or Cecil Fielder or Ryne Sandburg makes *per game*.

No. My one regret is that my teams won only one pennant, the Cleveland Indians in 1948. A player's—and a manager's—first World Series is like a child's first taste of ice cream. It's never enough.

I'm sorry I never got to another World Series—with the Indians or Boston or the Kansas City Athletics or the Chicago Cubs. It's something I'll always regret.

But more than that, I'm grateful to the Lord for giving me the ability to play the wonderful game of baseball, and that I was never seriously injured and could continue to make the most of the ability with which I was blessed.

I enjoyed my playing and managing career, as I did my 30 years in radio. I could not have asked for better people to be associated with, especially Jack Brickhouse and Jack Rosenberg, who were the first to believe I could do the job on WGN, and Jack Quinlan and Vince Lloyd, who shared their microphones with

me and never found fault with my grammar or sentence structure or vocabulary, not even my inability to pronounce rhododendron (at least I can spell it).

I am grateful to them, as I always will be to Dr. J. D. Logsdon,
my first baseball and basketball coach, who was the superintendent at Whittier Elementary School in Harvey; Jack Lipe, my
baseball coach and the athletic director at Thornton Township
High School; and my coaches at the University of Illinois, Doug
Mills and Wally Roettger, all of whom taught me the importance
of fair play, team play, and the determination to excel.

My father, Louis Boudreau, played the major role in developing my ability and nurturing my interest in baseball. While I
thank the Lord that Dad lived long enough to know that I had
made it to the big leagues, I'm sorry he wasn't there to share my
success and to appreciate, as I did, my election to the Hall of
Fame.

I also owe the fans of Cleveland a large debt of gratitude for
their loyalty throughout my career with the Indians, especially in
those dark days during the winter of 1947-48, when Bill Veeck
was determined to trade me.

Without their support I would have been playing for the St.
Louis Browns in 1948, the most wonderful year of my life, when
everything came together for the Indians, the city of Cleveland,
and me.

Most of all I'm grateful to my wife Della, who raised our four
children—Barbara, Sharon, Lou and Jim—pretty much by her-
self while I was on the road during my playing and managing
career, and after I went into broadcasting.

Della was always there, and whatever I wanted, she wanted,
too. I am fortunate to have a wife who understood and believed
in me even before that day in June 1938 when we were two scared
kids standing before a Justice of the Peace in Wheeler, Indiana.

The finishing touches to a wonderful career were applied
after I retired from WGN and stepped out of the limelight. More
than four hundred of my friends in Harvey had a "night" for me
in 1992, during which they thanked me.

Imagine that. Thanking me when I'm the one who had all the
fun and has all those wonderful stored-up memories.

There were too many who put together that night to name
individually, but I feel compelled to put into writing my appre-

ciation to the members of the committee: Bill Augustus, Dick Bauer, Tom Dreesen, Ron Ferguson, Don King, Bill Kolloway, Mark Lacey, George Perry, Don Morrison, Bill Purden, John Sullivan, and Richard Taylor.

I often go downstairs to my recreation room just to look at the awards and the trophies I've won and to contemplate my good fortune. I was in most of the right places, most of the time. It was a good career.

And if I had it all to do over again, there's nothing I'd change. Not a thing, including—*especially*—that letter I wrote back on November 20, 1941, to Alva Bradley, applying for the job as manager of the Cleveland Indians.

Lou Boudreau Statistics

Year	Team	League	Pos.	G.	BA	AB	H	2B	3B	HR	R	RBI	BB	SO	FA
1938	Cedar Rapids	Three-I	3B	60	.290	231	67	13	4	3	56	20	25	14	.935
1938	Cleveland	Amer.	3B	1	.000	1	0	0	0	0	0	0	1	0	.000
1939	Buffalo	Int.	SS	115	.331	481	159	32	7	17	88	57	37	34	.941
1939	Cleveland	Amer.	SS	53	.258	225	58	15	4	0	42	19	28	24	.953
1940	Cleveland	Amer.	SS	155	.295	627	185	46	10	9	97	101	73	39	.968
1941	Cleveland	Amer.	SS	148	.257	579	149	45	8	10	95	56	85	57	.966
1942	Cleveland	Amer.	SS	147	.283	506	143	18	10	2	57	58	75	39	.965
1943	Cleveland	Amer.	SS-C	152	.286	539	154	32	7	3	69	67	90	31	.970
1944	Cleveland	Amer.	SS-C	150	.327	584	191	45	5	3	91	67	73	39	.978
1945	Cleveland	Amer.	SS	97	.306	346	106	24	1	3	50	48	35	20	.983
1946	Cleveland	Amer.	SS	140	.293	515	151	30	6	6	51	62	40	14	.970
1947	Cleveland	Amer.	SS	150	.307	538	165	45	3	4	79	67	67	10	.982
1948	Cleveland	Amer.	SS-C	152	.355	560	199	33	6	18	116	106	98	9	.975
1949	Cleveland	Amer.	SS-3B	134	.284	475	135	20	3	4	53	60	70	10	.981
1950	Cleveland	Amer.	1B-2B, SS-3B	81	.269	260	70	13	2	1	23	29	31	5	.988
1951	Boston	Amer.	1B-2B, SS-3B	82	.267	273	73	18	1	5	37	47	30	12	.948
1952	Boston	Amer.	1B, SS-3B	4	.000	2	0	0	0	0	1	2	0	0	1.000
Major League Totals				1,646	.295	6,030	1,779	385	66	68	861	789	796	309	.973

World Series

Year	Team	League	Pos.	G.	BA	AB	H	2B	3B	HR	R	RBI	BB	SO	FA
1948	Cleveland	Amer.	SS	6	.273	22	6	4	0	0	1	3	1	1	1.000

All-Star Games

	Pos.	BA	AB	H	2B	3B	HR	R	RBI	BB	SO	FA
1940	SS	.000	0	0	0	0	0	0	0	0	0	.000
1941	SS	1.000	2	2	0	0	0	0	1	0	0	1.000
1942	SS	.250	4	1	0	0	1	1	1	0	0	1.000
1943	DNP											
1944	DNP											
1947	SS	.250	4	1	0	0	0	0	0	0	1	1.000
1948	SS	.000	2	0	0	0	0	0	1	0	0	1.000
Totals		**.333**	**12**	**4**	**0**	**0**	**1**	**1**	**3**	**0**	**1**	**1.000**

Managerial Record

Year	Team	Won	Lost	Pct.	Finish	GB
1942	Cleveland	75	79	.487	4	28
1943	Cleveland	82	71	.536	3	15 1/2
1944	Cleveland	72	82	.468	5	17
1945	Cleveland	73	72	.503	5	11
1946	Cleveland	68	86	.442	6	36
1947	Cleveland	80	74	.519	4	17
1948	Cleveland	97	58	.626	1	-
1949	Cleveland	89	65	.578	3	8
1950	Cleveland	92	62	.597	4	6
1952	Boston	76	78	.494	6	19
1953	Boston	84	69	.549	4	16
1954	Boston	69	85	.448	4	42
1955	Kansas City	63	91	.409	6	33
1956	Kansas City	52	102	.338	8	45
1957	Kansas City	36	67	.350	8	38 1/2
1960	Chicago Cubs	54	83	.394	8	35
16 Seasons		**1,162**	**1,224**	**.487**		

Awards and Accomplishments
• American League Most Valuable Player Award in 1948
• Managed American League to victory in the 1949 All-Star Game
• Uniform number 5 retired by Thorton Township High School, University of Illinois, and Cleveland Indians
• American League batting championship with .327 average in 1944
• Led American League shortstops in fielding percentage eight years, a record held jointly with Everett Scott (1914-26)